Learning from
Multiple Social Networks

Synthesis Lectures on Information Concepts, Retrieval, and Services

Editor
Gary Marchionini, *University of North Carolina, Chapel Hill*

Synthesis Lectures on Information Concepts, Retrieval, and Services publishes short books on topics pertaining to information science and applications of technology to information discovery, production, distribution, and management. Potential topics include: data models, indexing theory and algorithms, classification, information architecture, information economics, privacy and identity, scholarly communication, bibliometrics and webometrics, personal information management, human information behavior, digital libraries, archives and preservation, cultural informatics, information retrieval evaluation, data fusion, relevance feedback, recommendation systems, question answering, natural language processing for retrieval, text summarization, multimedia retrieval, multilingual retrieval, and exploratory search.

Learning from Multiple Social Networks
Liqiang Nie, Xuemeng Song, and Tat-Seng Chua

ISBN: 978-3-031-01172-6   paperback
ISBN: 978-3-031-02300-2   ebook

DOI 10.1007/978-3-031-02300-2

A Publication in the Springer series
SYNTHESIS LECTURES ON INFORMATION CONCEPTS, RETRIEVAL, AND SERVICES

Lecture #48
Series Editor: Gary Marchionini, *University of North Carolina, Chapel Hill*
Series ISSN
Print 1947-945X   Electronic 1947-9468

Learning from
Multiple Social Networks

Liqiang Nie, Xuemeng Song, and Tat-Seng Chua
National University of Singapore

*SYNTHESIS LECTURES ON INFORMATION CONCEPTS, RETRIEVAL,
AND SERVICES #48*

ABSTRACT

With the proliferation of social network services, more and more social users, such as individuals and organizations, are simultaneously involved in multiple social networks for various purposes. In fact, multiple social networks characterize the same social users from different perspectives, and their contexts are usually consistent or complementary rather than independent. Hence, as compared to using information from a single social network, appropriate aggregation of multiple social networks offers us a better way to comprehensively understand the given social users.

Learning across multiple social networks brings opportunities to new services and applications as well as new insights on user online behaviors, yet it raises tough challenges: (1) How can we map different social network accounts to the same social users? (2) How can we complete the item-wise and block-wise missing data? (3) How can we leverage the relatedness among sources to strengthen the learning performance? And (4) How can we jointly model the dual-heterogeneities: multiple tasks exist for the given application and each task has various features from multiple sources? These questions have been largely unexplored to date.

We noticed this timely opportunity, and in this book we present some state-of-the-art theories and novel practical applications on aggregation of multiple social networks. In particular, we first introduce multi-source dataset construction. We then introduce how to effectively and efficiently complete the item-wise and block-wise missing data, which are caused by the inactive social users in some social networks. We next detail the proposed multi-source mono-task learning model and its application in volunteerism tendency prediction. As a counterpart, we also present a mono-source multi-task learning model and apply it to user interest inference. We seamlessly unify these models with the so-called multi-source multi-task learning, and demonstrate several application scenarios, such as occupation prediction. Finally, we conclude the book and figure out the future research directions in multiple social network learning, including the privacy issues and source complementarity modeling.

This is preliminary research on learning from multiple social networks, and we hope it can inspire more active researchers to work on this exciting area. If we have seen further it is by standing on the shoulders of giants.

KEYWORDS

multiple social networks, missing data, data completion, multi-source mono-task learning, mono-source multi-task learning, multi-source multi-task learning, volunteerism tendency prediction, user interest mining, occupation inference, career path modeling, user attribute learning

Contents

Acknowledgments

This book would not have been completed, or at least not what it looks like now, without the support, direction and help of many people. It is a pleasure to take this opportunity to acknowledge those who made substantial contributions in various ways to this time-consuming book project.

Our first and foremost thanks undoubtedly goes to the members of Lab for Media Search.[1] We discussed with them some technical sections of the book. Their constructive feedback and comments at various stages have been significantly helpful in shaping the book up to completion. Most importantly, they made this book project enjoyable. Particular thanks go to Mr. Xiang Wang who read the earlier drafts of the manuscript and provided helpful comments to improve the readability. Meanwhile, Mr. Xiang Wang is the major contributor of Chapter 4 in this book.

We are very grateful to the anonymous reviewers. Despite their busy schedules, they read the book very carefully and gave us many insightful suggestions.

On the publication side, we would like to express our heartfelt gratitude to the editor, Dr. Gary Marchionini, and the executive editor, Ms. Diane Cerra. They managed to get everything done on time and provided us with many pieces of valuable advice.

Lastly, our thanks would be reserved to our beloved families for their selfless consideration, endless love and unconditional support. We dedicate this book to them, with deep love.

Liqiang Nie, Xuemeng Song, and Tat-Seng Chua
March 2016

---

[1]http://lms.comp.nus.edu.sg/

CHAPTER 1

Introduction

1.1 BACKGROUND

We are living in the era of social networks, which connect and organize social actors, such as individuals and organizations, throughout the world. Yet, an increasing number of social actors are involved in multiple social networks at the same time. This trend has been statistically reflected in a recent survey[1] as shown in Figure 1.1: multi-platform use is on the rise. In particular, more than half of Internet adult users (52%) in 2014 use two or more of the social media sites measured

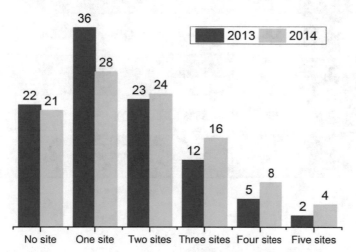

Figure 1.1: Statistics of multi-platform social media use in year 2013 and 2014.

---

[1]http://heidicohen.com/multi-platform-social-media-use/

(Facebook,[2] Twitter,[3] Instagram,[4] Pinterest,[5] and LinkedIn[6]) compared with 42% who did so in 2013. In addition, this survey also reported that teens are diversifying their social network site use, and a majority of teens (71%) are concurrently using more than one social site. This survey was conducted by the Pew Research Center.[7]

Besides the macro-survey result, Pew Research Center also reported a micro-survey result as summarized in Table 1.1: the percentage of users of each particular site who use another particular site. The following observations can be made from this table: (1) Facebook remains the most popular platform. A significant majority of Twitter, Instagram, Pinterest and LinkedIn users also use Facebook, more frequently than any other site. At the low end, 86% of LinkedIn users are also on Facebook. At the high end, 94% of Instagram users use Facebook. (2) Turning to sites other than Facebook, a significant level of overlap exists between Instagram and Twitter users; 58% of Twitter users also use Instagram, and 52% of Instagram users also use Twitter. Among non-Facebook sites, this is the highest rate of "reciprocity" between user groups measured.

Table 1.1: Illustration of social media matrix among five popular social network sites

	Use Twitter	Use Instagram	Use Pinterest	Use LinkedIn	Use Facebook
% of Twitter users who use...	–	58%	42%	47%	91%
% of Instagram users who use...	52%	–	47%	38%	94%
% of Pinterest users who use...	34%	43%	–	40%	88%
% of LinkedIn users who use...	39%	35%	40%	–	86%
% of Facebook users who use...	29%	34%	34%	33%	–

[2]https://www.facebook.com/
[3]https://twitter.com/
[4]https://instagram.com/
[5]https://www.pinterest.com/
[6]https://www.linkedin.com/
[7]The Pew Research Center is a nonpartisan American think tank based in Washington, D.C., that provides information on social issues, public opinion, and demographic trends shaping the United States and the world. It conducts public opinion polling, demographic research, media content analysis, and other empirical social science research. It does not take explicit policy positions. It is a subsidiary of The Pew Charitable Trusts.

1.2   MOTIVATION

In fact, multiple social networks essentially characterize the same social actors from different perspectives. For example, Twitter reflects users' casual activities and personal opinions; Foursquare[8]
shares users' footprints with their friends; Facebook explicitly exposes users' social connections
and daily events; while LinkedIn uncovers users' professional skills and career paths. These heterogeneous information cues distributed in diverse social networks are usually consistent or complementary to each other rather than mutually conflicting.

Hence, as compared to a single social network, appropriate aggregation of data from multiple social networks provides us a better way to comprehensively understand the given social
actors. Beyond the traditional early fusion [54, 110] and late fusion [33, 117, 127], appropriate aggregation should explore the relatedness among sources and should mutually reinforce each
single source. Learning from multiple social networks is hence the basis to boost the accuracy performance of many applications. For example, we can learn descriptive user representation, build
predictive models for user profiles, and recommend prescriptive actions based on complete historical behaviors. Therefore, effective techniques for multiple social network learning are highly
desired.

1.3   CHALLENGES

Despite of its significant value, effectively unifying and uncovering the information embedded in
heterogeneous social sites remains a largely unaddressed research problem. To be more specific,
it still suffers from the following challenges:

- Social accounts alignment. A social actor may be concurrently involved in multiple platforms
  with different user names or user IDs. How can we map different social network accounts
  to the same social users?

- Missing data issues. Another challenge we face is the item-wise and block-wise missing
  data problem. Although some users have multiple social accounts on different social networks, generally they are active on only a few of them. One simple approach to address
  this challenge is to discard all the incomplete subjects. It is apparent that this approach will
  dramatically reduce the training size, thereby resulting in over-fitting in the model learning
  stage. Therefore, accurately completing missing data by jointly utilizing multiple sources and
  fully making use of available information is a necessity to enhance the learning performance.

- Source fusion. Several research efforts have been dedicated to source fusion. They can be
  roughly classified into two major categories: early fusion and late fusion. Early fusion methods, such as [110], merge all extracted features from different sources or modalities into
  a single concatenated feature vector to construct a joint feature space. Thereby, machine

---

[8]https://foursquare.com/

learning approaches can be further applied. However, they may suffer from the following limitations. First, they are unable to differentiate and leverage the discrimination power of distinct sources. Second, the features extracted from various sources may not fall into the same semantic space. Simply merging all features actually brings in a certain extent of noise and ambiguity. Third, they may lead to the curse of dimensionality since the final feature vector would be of very high dimension, and the number of data instances required will increase exponentially. On the other hand, late fusion, such as [127], analyzes each source separately and then integrates their results. The fused result however might not be reasonably accurate for two reasons. First, each feature space might not be sufficiently descriptive to represent the complex semantics of the social actors. Therefore, separate results would be suboptimal and the integration may not result in a desired outcome. Second, it is labor-intensive to tune the fusion weights for different source views. Even worse, the optimal parameters for one application cannot be directly applied to another one. Basically, different aspects of users are revealed in different social networks and all these aspects tend to characterize the essences of the same users. Formally, data from multi-sources describe the same user and thus the results predicted by different sources should be similar. Therefore, it is expected to take the source confidence and source consistency into consideration.

- Dual-heterogeneities. In practice, there exists multiple related tasks for the same application. Take the application of user interest inference as an example. Given a set of interests $\mathcal{I} = \{basketball, football, travel, cooking\}$, the relatedness between *basketball* and *football* may be stronger than that between *basketball* and *cooking*. Each interest is usually aligned with one task and the tasks of interests are inter-correlated in a complex way rather than independent to each other. On the other hand, each task has features from multiple sources. However, far too little attention has been paid to jointly consider the dual-heterogeneities.

In addition, several other challenges have been raised, for example, temporal progression modeling and complementary relationships among sources. It is worth mentioning that a wide range of existing approaches have been proposed and applied to process and analyze single social networks separately, with solid theoretical underpinnings and practical success. However, few of them take multiple social networks into consideration simultaneously. As such, they overlook the inter-relations among sources and are unable to fully address the aforementioned problems.

1.4   OUR SOLUTIONS AND APPLICATIONS

We noticed these timely opportunities, and in this book we present some state-of-the-art theories and novel applications on multiple social networks. In particular, we first describe how to gather and complete multi-source datasets. With the help of some social sites, we can easily map various social network accounts to the same social actors, and infer the item-wise and block-wise missing data by making full use of the available data.

We then detail the proposed multiple social network learning model, which co-regularizes the source confidence and consistency. We empirically evaluate this proposed model on the application of volunteerism tendency prediction. Volunteers have always been in urgent need for nonprofit organizations to sustain their continuing operations. However, it is expensive and time consuming to recruit volunteers using traditional approaches. In the Web 2.0 era, the abundant and ubiquitous social media data open a door to the possibility of automatic volunteer identification. We aim to fully explore this possibility by predicting users' volunteerism tendency from user-generated content collected from multiple social networks.

Beyond binary classifications of two possible states, applications with more than two classes are very common, such as user interest inference. Most of the traditional multi-task learning models frequently treat each category as one task, and assume that all the tasks are related. This assumption does not always hold in some real-world contexts, and hence may lead to negative transfer among dissimilar tasks. As a remedy, clustered multi-task learning has emerged to constrain task sharing within the same clusters. But it still remains in its infancy due to the inefficient solutions and pre-specified parameters. We present a novel and efficient clustered multi-task learning model, which automatically discovers the underlying grouping structure of tasks. Based on this structure, the global, inter-group, and intra-group relatedness among tasks are jointly regularized to maximize the data sharing. Most importantly, a closed-form solution has been demonstrated to boost the efficient performance. The proposed model has been applied to an application on user interest mining from social media. Extensive experimental results on a public dataset have demonstrated its superiority in efficacy and efficiency over the state-of-the-arts competitors. The code and data have been released to facilitate further research by the research community.

Many real-world applications in the era of multiple social networks frequently exhibit dual-heterogeneities: each task has features from multiple sources, and multiple tasks are related with each other in a complex way. To address such problems, we propose a series of unified models to jointly consider the source and task relatedness. To be more specific, the disagreements among predicted results from each single source are penalized, and the relatedness among tasks is encoded into a predefined structure. We applied these models to some users' attributes learning applications, comprising of users' interest inference, occupation prediction, as well as career path modeling.

We finally conclude the book and discuss various fascinating problems that remain open, such as the privacy issues and source complementarity modeling.

1.5 OUTLINE OF THIS BOOK

This book presents an in-depth introduction to multiple social network learning problems, and a comprehensive survey of all the important research topics and latest developments in the field. It is suitable for students, researchers, and practitioners who are interested in multiple social network analysis.

The remainder of this book consists of five chapters. Chapter 2 introduces the approaches to data gathering and illustrates some representative approaches to data completion. Chapter 3 describes formally a general scheme of multiple social network learning and presents its corresponding application of volunteerism tendency prediction. This is a binary classification application. In Chapter 4, we present a novel multi-task learning model to handle the multi-class problems. In Chapter 5, we extend the mono-source or mono-task learning models to a multi-source multi-task learning model. We theoretically derive its closed-form solution and practically apply it to the interest inference application. In Chapter 6, we present the variant of multi-task multi-source learning model, which is able to learn the task-specific and task-sharing features. To derive its analytical solution, we relax this model to a smooth and convex function. We verify this model over the applications of occupation inference and career path modeling. We conclude this book and figure out the future research directions in Chapter 7.

CHAPTER 2

Data Gathering and Completion

2.1 USER ACCOUNTS ALIGNMENT

To represent the same users with multiple sources, we need to first tackle the problem of "Social Account Mapping," which aims to align the same users across different social networks by linking their multiple social accounts [1]. However, users may have different usernames in different social networks, making the linkage task difficult [135]. In the past few years, the research on user profile linkage has developed in parallel with the rapid development of online social networks, which can be roughly divided into three categories. The methods in the first category compare the similarity between two profiles, usually one from one social network and one from another, by carefully exploring their social posts and attributes, such as their name, gender, email, and location [39, 51, 72, 78, 116, 131, 132]. However, users' profiles oftentimes are not available, and sometimes are inaccurate. To address this problem, the approaches in the second category, aside from content-based comparison, leverage users' social connections to identify their social accounts. The basic philosophy is that users often have similar social connections in different online social networks [63, 114]. However, the computation cost is extremely large when considering the connections in the whole network, and the early errors often get amplified. Most recently, efforts in the third category focus on integrating the social connections and social content to boost the performance of user profiles linkage [73, 138]. However, they are still in the infant stage.

To accurately establish this alignment, in this work, we leverage the emerging social services such as About.me[1] and Quora,[2] where they encourage users to explicitly list their multiple social accounts on one profile. Take About.me as an example. The site offers registered users a convenient platform to link multiple online identities, relevant external sites, and popular social networking websites such as Foursquare, Instagram, LinkedIn, Twitter, and Flickr.[3] It is characterized by its one-page user profiles, each with a large and artistic background image and abbreviated biography. Figure 2.1 shows the screenshots of profiles of a user on About.me and Quora, respectively. From these screenshots, we can see that the bottom of each profile displays a list of external links to this user's other social networks. With such accesses, we can harvest users' distributed social contents from multiple social networks.

---

[1]https://about.me/
[2]https://www.quora.com/
[3]https://www.flickr.com/

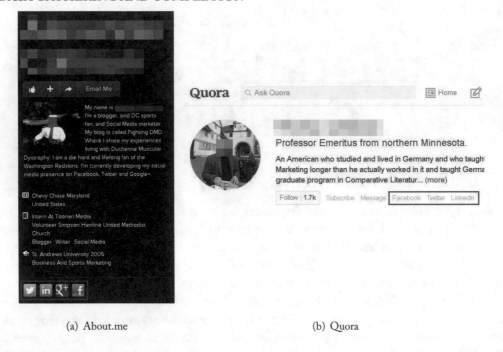

(a) About.me   (b) Quora

Figure 2.1: Structure illustration of social accounts alignment in both About.me and Quora. The icons in the red dotted rectangle are links to other social accounts of the same user. To avoid leakage of private information, we deliberately partially cover the name and contact information.

2.2   MISSING DATA PROBLEMS

In reality, not all users are active enough on all the given social networks. This frequently leads to a block-wise data missing problem. In particular, we treat a user as missing on Twitter or Facebook if this user has fewer than 10 historical social posts on that site. In addition, due to the absence of social post mechanism in LinkedIn, we treat a user as missing in LinkedIn if the word count of this user's profile is less than 50. Figure 2.2 shows the statistics of data incompletion based on 5,436 users.[4] As can be seen, about 50% of users have complete data from all three social networks; 1% and 47% of users have missing data from either Facebook and LinkedIn; while 2% of the users have missing data of both sites.

On the other hand, a significant body of Internet users might be reluctant to expose their attributes to the public, due to various concerns of privacy and security issues. This causes the item-wise missing problem. The statistics of profile completeness of users over various social networks are shown in Figure 2.3, based on our pilot study of 172,235 users. From this figure, we have the following observations: (1) 56.2% of users provide their education details in Facebook

---

[4]These users are crawled for the application of volunteerism tendency prediction, which will be introduced in the next chapter.

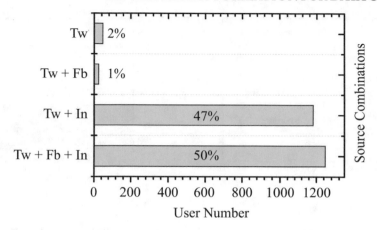

Figure 2.2: Statistics of the incomplete data. Tw: Users with Twitter data only; Tw+Fb: Users with Twitter and Facebook data only; Tw+In: Users with Twitter and Linkedin data only; Tw+Fb+In: Users without missing data.

profiles, while 81% of LinkedIn users provide their school information. The incompleteness hinders the effective similarity estimation based on users' profile data; (2) The data distributed in different social networks are complementary. For example, Facebook profiles provide users' gender information but fail to present the bio descriptions for users, which is alternatively given by Twitter profiles. Hence, integration of users' information distributed in various social networks is essential to derive complete user profiles. As a by-product, leveraging multiple sources increases the robustness, helps to handle the cold start problem [104], and may be beneficial to other applications, such as recommendations.

2.3   MATRIX FACTORIZATION FOR DATA COMPLETION

The following approaches can be employed to handle the data missing problem:

- **Remove**: This approach simply removes the users with missing items or missing sources.

- **Zero**: We assigned zero value to any element that is missing. When the data are normalized to have zero mean with unit standard deviation, this is equivalent to mean value imputation [129].

- **Average**: This method imputes the missing features with the average values of the corresponding feature items.

- **KNN**: The k-nearest neighbor method replaces the missing value in the data matrix with the corresponding value from the nearest column. The Gaussian kernel function [84] can be employed to estimate the pair-wise similarity.

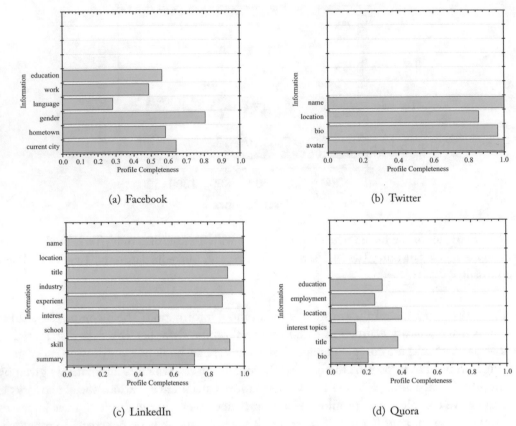

(a) Facebook   (b) Twitter

(c) LinkedIn   (d) Quora

Figure 2.3: Profile completeness of users over four prevailing social networks.

However, the first approach frequently leads to information loss, as users with partial available data are removed. Meanwhile, it dramatically reduces the size of training data, which is prone to a suboptimal model. The second method cannot leverage any available context to infer the missing values. The last two methods do explore the local neighbor information, but overlook how well the completed matrix approximates the original one globally.

On the other hand, matrix factorization is fully competent for this task, which is able to discover the latent features underlying the interactions between two different kinds of entities, such as users and products they are rating on, and is popular in collaborative recommendation systems [65, 76, 142, 146].

Before stepping into the matrix factorization techniques, we first describe some notations, which are universally applicable to the entire book. In particular, we use bold capital letters (e.g., $\mathbf{X}$) and bold lowercase letters (e.g., $\mathbf{x}$) to denote matrices and vectors, respectively. We employ non-bold letters (e.g., x) to represent scalars, and Greek letters (e.g., λ) as parameters. If not clarified, all vectors are in column forms.

Formally, we denote $\mathbf{M} = [\mathbf{X_1}, \mathbf{X_2}, ..., \mathbf{X_S}, \mathbf{Y}] \in \mathbb{R}^{N \times D}$, where $D = T + \sum_s^S D_s$. $\mathbf{X_s}$ and $\mathbf{Y}$ respectively refer to all users on the s-th source and their labels of T categories. Our target is to seek for two matrices $\mathbf{P} \in \mathbb{R}^{N \times L}$ and $\mathbf{Q} \in \mathbb{R}^{L \times D}$ such that their product approximates $\mathbf{M}$,

$$\mathbf{M} \approx \hat{\mathbf{M}} = \mathbf{P} \times \mathbf{Q}. \tag{2.1}$$

where matrix $\mathbf{Q}$ is the basis matrix in the latent space, and matrix $\mathbf{P}$ is the latent representation of users in the latent space. The above equation can be intuitively interpreted as follows: the observed instances can be generated by additive combination of underlying set of hidden basis.

To obtain the estimated value $\hat{M}_{ij}$, we multiply the i-th row of $\mathbf{P}$ and j-th column of $\mathbf{Q}$. We have

$$\hat{M}_{ij} = \sum_{r=1}^{L} P_{ir} Q_{rj}. \tag{2.2}$$

The bias between all the estimated and true values over all non-missing items is formulated as,

$$\epsilon = \sum_{ij} e_{ij}^2 + \frac{\gamma}{2} \left(\| \mathbf{P} \|^2 + \| \mathbf{Q} \|^2 \right) \tag{2.3}$$

$$= \sum_{i}^{n} \sum_{j}^{d} \left(M_{ij} - \hat{M}_{ij} \right)^2 + \frac{\gamma}{2} \left(\| \mathbf{P} \|^2 + \| \mathbf{Q} \|^2 \right),$$

where the regularization is incorporated to avoid overfitting, and $\gamma > 0$ is a regularization parameter.

A general algorithm for minimizing the objective function ϵ is gradient descent. For our problem, gradient descent leads to the following additive update rules,

$$\begin{cases} P_{ir}^{(t+1)} = P_{ir}^{(t)} - \alpha \frac{\partial \epsilon}{\partial P_{ir}} \\ Q_{rj}^{(t+1)} = Q_{rj}^{(t)} - \alpha \frac{\partial \epsilon}{\partial Q_{rj}}, \end{cases} \tag{2.4}$$

where the derivative results are,

$$\begin{cases} \frac{\partial \epsilon}{\partial P_{ir}} = -2 \left(M_{ij} - \hat{M}_{ij} \right) Q_{rj} + \gamma P_{ir} \\ \frac{\partial \epsilon}{\partial Q_{rj}} = -2 \left(M_{ij} - \hat{M}_{ij} \right) P_{ir} + \gamma Q_{rj}, \end{cases} \tag{2.5}$$

where α is the learning rate. One intuitive solution for the choice of learning rate is to have a constant rate. As long as α is sufficiently small, the above updates should reduce ϵ unless $\mathbf{P}$ and $\mathbf{Q}$ are at a stationary point. However, it will take a long time to converge. Another simple rule of thumb is to decrease the learning rate over time, $\frac{\alpha_0}{1+\tau}$, where α_0 and τ are respectively the initial learning rate and the number of epoches. However, they all suffer from the sensitivity of initializations. To tackle such problems, we can implement an adaptive learning rate adjuster to monitor and adjust the learning rate α. This adjuster is triggered on each epoch. It will shrink the learning rate if the objective value goes up. The idea is that in this case the learning algorithm is overshooting the bottom of the objective function. On the other hand, the adjuster will increase the learning rate if the objective value decreases too slowly. This makes our learning rate parameter less important to the initialized value. Though it is not a very mathematically principled approach, it works well in practice. The matrix factorization method can be utilized to complete the element-wise and block-wise missing data.

2.4 MULTIPLE SOCIAL NETWORKS DATA COMPLETION

In this section, we propose an approach for multiple social network data completion (MSNDC). It is specifically designed for the block-wise data missing problem.

Suppose we have S data sources in total and each sample has at least one data source available. We employ the subset $\mathcal{C}_i \subseteq \mathcal{C}$ to indicate the presence of each source and the signature of a specific social network combination. Based on these combinations, all the data samples can be split into multiple exclusive sets, where each set corresponds to a combination. Figure 2.4 illustrates the incomplete data problem in our dataset, where SN_i denotes the i-th social network. As can be seen, all users have complete features from SN_1, while some users come with missing data in SN_2 or SN_3. Therefore, our dataset can be split into four exclusive social network combinations: $\mathcal{C}_1 = \{1, 2\}, \mathcal{C}_2 = \{1, 2, 3\}, \mathcal{C}_3 = \{1, 3\}, \mathcal{C}_4 = \{1\}$.

Inspired by [70], we use Non-negative Matrix Factorization (NMF) to explore the latent spaces that are shared by different social networks, and further infer the missing data based upon these latent spaces. It is reasonable to assume that the data from different social networks about the same user share certain latent features. We employ $\mathbf{X}_s^{\mathcal{C}_i} \in \mathbb{R}^{N_{c_i} \times D_s}$ to denote the samples generated from the s-th social network. It only contains samples that are available in the set of social networks $\mathcal{C}_i$, where $N_{\mathcal{C}_i}$ stands for the number of these samples. We use $\mathbf{U}_s \in \mathbb{R}^{z \times D_s}$ to represent the latent basis matrix for the s-th social network, and $\mathbf{P}_s^{\mathcal{C}_i} \in \mathbb{R}^{N_{c_i} \times z}$ to denote the corresponding latent representation of feature matrix $\mathbf{X}_s^{\mathcal{C}_i}$. z is the dimension of the shared latent space of different social networks. The intuitive assumption is that for the samples available in both the s-th and s'-th social networks, their corresponding latent representations should also be quite similar. In particular, we impose this constraint to NMF as follows,

$$\mathbf{P}_s^{\mathcal{C}_i} = \mathbf{P}_{s'}^{\mathcal{C}_i} = \mathbf{P}^{\mathcal{C}_i}, \tag{2.6}$$

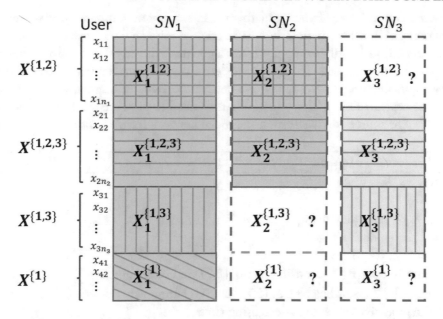

Figure 2.4: Illustration of the incomplete data from three sources. $\mathbf{X}_s^{\mathcal{C}_i}$ denotes the samples from social network s that are only available in the social network combination of $\mathcal{C}_i$.

where $s \neq s'$, $s \in \mathcal{C}_i$, and $s' \in \mathcal{C}_i$. We thus learn the shared subspaces by the following objective function,

$$
\begin{aligned}
\min_{\substack{\mathbf{U}_s \geq 0 \\ \mathbf{P}_s \geq 0}} & \left\| \begin{bmatrix} \mathbf{X}_1^{\{1\}} \\ \mathbf{X}_1^{\{1,2\}} \\ \mathbf{X}_1^{\{1,3\}} \\ \mathbf{X}_1^{\{1,2,3\}} \end{bmatrix} - \begin{bmatrix} \mathbf{P}^{\{1\}} \\ \mathbf{P}^{\{1,2\}} \\ \mathbf{P}^{\{1,3\}} \\ \mathbf{P}^{\{1,2,3\}} \end{bmatrix} \mathbf{U}_1 \right\|^2 + v \left\| \mathbf{P}_1 \right\|_1 + \eta \left\| \mathbf{U}_1 \right\|_1 \\
+ & \left\| \begin{bmatrix} \mathbf{X}_2^{\{1,2\}} \\ \mathbf{X}_2^{\{1,2,3\}} \end{bmatrix} - \begin{bmatrix} \mathbf{P}^{\{1,2\}} \\ \mathbf{P}^{\{1,2,3\}} \end{bmatrix} \mathbf{U}_2 \right\|^2 + v \left\| \mathbf{P}_2 \right\|_1 + \eta \left\| \mathbf{U}_2 \right\|_1 \\
+ & \left\| \begin{bmatrix} \mathbf{X}_3^{\{1,3\}} \\ \mathbf{X}_3^{\{1,2,3\}} \end{bmatrix} - \begin{bmatrix} \mathbf{P}^{\{1,3\}} \\ \mathbf{P}^{\{1,2,3\}} \end{bmatrix} \mathbf{U}_3 \right\|^2 + v \left\| \mathbf{P}_3 \right\|_1 + \eta \left\| \mathbf{U}_3 \right\|_1,
\end{aligned}
\tag{2.7}
$$

where v and η are the nonnegative tradeoff parameters for the regularizations. Similarly, we employ the alternating optimization strategy to solve the optimization in Eq. (2.7). To be more specific, we first initialize $\mathbf{U}_s$ and compute the optimal $\mathbf{P}_s$. Afterward, $\mathbf{P}_s$ is updated based on the computed $\mathbf{U}_s$. We keep this iterative procedure until the objective function converges.

The proposed approach differs from [70] in the following three aspects. First, it is generalized to handle the more challenging case where data samples are extracted from more than two social networks. Second, apart from regulating the latent representation matrix, we regularize the latent basis matrix. Third, we further derive the original missing data from the latent representation, where the authors in [70] just apply cluster algorithms directly to the latent representation of data instead of the original data. The reason we derive the missing data from latent representation is due to two considerations. One is that we believe the value of original known data is higher than the latent representation. The other is that we need to preserve the heterogeneities among data from different sources to fit our multiple social network learning models.

Algorithm 1 Alternative optimization for solving Eq. (2.7)

Input: $\mathbf{X}_1, \mathbf{X}_2, \mathbf{X}_3, \nu, \eta$
Output: $\hat{\mathbf{X}}$

1: Initialize $\mathbf{U}_s^{(0)}$ according to Eq. (2.8).
2: **for** $k = 1, 2, \cdots$ **do**
3:      **for** $s = 1, 2, \cdots, S$ **do**
4:          Compute each $\mathbf{P}_s^{(k)}$ according to Eq. (2.7) via GCD approach.
5:          Update $\mathbf{U}_s^{(k)}$ according to Eq. (2.7) via GCD approach.
6:          **if** the objective value stops decreasing **then**
7:              return $\mathbf{U}_s = \mathbf{U}_s^{(k)}$ and $\mathbf{P}_s = \mathbf{P}_s^{(k)}$
8:          **end if**
9:      **end for**
10: **end for**
11: **for** $j = 1, 2, \cdots, S$ **do**
12:     **for** $\mathcal{C}_q \subseteq \mathcal{C}$ **do**
13:         **if** $j \in \mathcal{C}_q$ **then**
14:             $\hat{\mathbf{X}}_j^{\mathcal{C}_q} = \mathbf{X}_j^{\mathcal{C}_q}$.
15:         **else**
16:             Infer $\hat{\mathbf{X}}_j^{\mathcal{C}_q}$ according to Eq. (2.9).
17:         **end if**
18:     **end for**
19: **end for**

In order to increase the efficiency of the iterative procedure, we initialize $\mathbf{U}_s$ by optimizing the following objective function,

$$
\begin{aligned}
\min_{\mathbf{U}_s \geq \mathbf{0}} & \left\| \mathbf{X}_1^{\{1,2,3\}} - \mathbf{P}^{\{1,2,3\}}\mathbf{U}_1 \right\|^2 + \nu \left\| \mathbf{P}^{\{1,2,3\}} \right\|_1 + \eta \left\| \mathbf{U}_1 \right\|_1 \\
& + \left\| \mathbf{X}_2^{\{1,2,3\}} - \mathbf{P}^{\{1,2,3\}}\mathbf{U}_2 \right\|^2 + \eta \left\| \mathbf{U}_2 \right\|_1 \\
& + \left\| \mathbf{X}_3^{\{1,2,3\}} - \mathbf{P}^{\{1,2,3\}}\mathbf{U}_3 \right\|^2 + \eta \left\| \mathbf{U}_3 \right\|_1 .
\end{aligned}
\tag{2.8}
$$

We then alternatively optimize $\mathbf{U}_s$ and $\mathbf{P}_s$ until the objective function converges. Specifically, we employ the greedy coordinate descent (GCD) approach [48], which has been found to be tremendously fast to solve NMF decomposition with L1-norm regularization. Finally, we obtain $\mathbf{P}_s, \mathbf{U}_s, s \in \mathcal{C}$, based on which we can infer the missing data as follows,

$$\hat{\mathbf{X}}_s^{\mathcal{C}_i} = \mathbf{P}^{\mathcal{C}_i} \mathbf{U}_s, \quad \forall s \notin \mathcal{C}_i. \tag{2.9}$$

Algorithm 1 summarizes the overall procedures for alternating optimization.

2.5 SUMMARY

This chapter presents the way of user accounts alignment and the strategies for data completion. In particular, we first summarize the existing methods on user accounts linkage over multiple social sites and point out their limitations. With the help of some social sites, such as Quora and About.me, we provide a reliable way of data gathering, which can perfectly avoid the limitations of the traditional methods and save computational cost. Following that, we explore the basic reasons of block-wise and item-wise data missing problems. Meanwhile, we introduce two matrix factorization style models to solve the missing data problems, which make full use of available data to boost the accuracy. The validations of these two models will be detailed in the following chapters.

CHAPTER 3

Multi-source Mono-task Learning

3.1 APPLICATION: VOLUNTEERISM TENDENCY PREDICTION

Volunteerism was defined in [93] as long-term, planned, prosocial behaviors that can benefit strangers and occur within organizational settings. Persons exhibiting volunteerism are the so-called volunteers, serving socially and economically as an important work force in modern society. According to [101], society would face a major crisis without volunteers, especially for nonprofit organizations (NPOs), since they are always in urgent need of volunteers to sustain their daily operations. Traditionally, it has been expensive and time consuming for NPOs to aimlessly recruit volunteers from huge crowd. It is thus highly desirable to develop an automatic volunteer identification system to alleviate the dilemma that a number of NPOs are facing [112].

In fact, several social researchers have paid attention to volunteerism analysis before the Web 2.0 era. These efforts are mainly based on survey data or related records of individuals' volunteer activities [119, 122]. Although great success has been achieved, these approaches suffer from the following two limitations. First, such approaches are hindered by limited and isolated samples as well as constrained individual characteristics. In particular, the experimental data are collected via questionnaires or face-to-face interviews, only small-scale dataset and certain basic demographic information, such as gender, marital status, and income, are available. Second, they mainly focus on the correlation analysis between volunteerism and such characteristics without quantitative volunteerism tendency prediction. For instance, the work in [94] found that users' volunteerism tendency can be affected by four factors: demographic characteristics, personal attributes, volunteer activators, and social pressure.

On the other hand, with the popularity of social media services, a large volume of user-generated content (UGCs) exist, which may reflect users' thoughts as well as opinions [88] and serve as sensors for users' attributes. Several efforts have been dedicated to research on the inference of users' attributes using these data. For example, some methods have been proposed to learn users' attributes such as gender, age, and personality from UGCs [95, 98]. As users' demographic information and personality play a vital role in users' volunteerism tendency [94], we believe that UGCs bear the potential to offer evidence as to the degree of a person's willingness in attending activities. This fact propels us to novelly explore users' distributed UGCs of multiple social networks to approach the volunteer identification problem.

However, the prediction of users' volunteerism tendency by taking advantage of UGCs from multiple social networks is nontrivial. First, it is not easy to generate a comprehensive overview of users from the multiple heterogeneous social networks. The information about users from a single social network is often limited and incomplete [1, 147]. Thanks to the different highlights of different services, people participate in multiple social networks for different purposes, and their casually distributed online data, especially from multiple social networks, which can comprehensively reveal users' personal concerns, interests [19, 108] and even personality traits [97, 98]. Consequently, aggregating all these different facets about users revealed by different social media services effectively is a challenging problem. Second, the real word dataset may contain block-wise missing data due to some users' inactivity in social networks during a certain period of time. Third, the specific task also brings us another issue in terms of data collection and ground truth construction. In addition, we have to extract a rich set of volunteer-oriented features to capture users' volunteerism tendency.

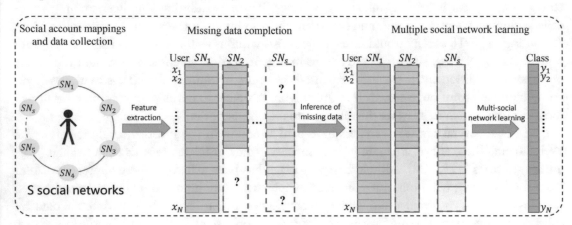

Figure 3.1: Illustration of our proposed scheme. We first collect and align users' distributed data from multiple social networks. We then jointly infer the block-wise missing data based on the available data. We finally apply our proposed model on the complete data. SN_i, x_j, and y_l refer to the i-th social network, j-th user sample, and the l-th corresponding label, respectively.

To address these problems, we present a scheme, which co-regulates the source confidence and source consistency. Figure 3.1 shows our proposed scheme comprising three components. Given a set of users, we first crawl their historical contents and all social connections. The first component extracts the multi-faceted information cues to describe a given user, including demographic information, practical behaviors, historical posts, and profiles of social connections. To deal with the block-wise missing data, the second component attempts to infer the block-wise missing data by learning a latent space shared by different social networks, achieving a complete input to the next component. We finally use the last component to conduct **MultIple S**ocial ne**T**work l**EaR**ning (MISTER) on the complete data. Particularly, we model the confidence of different data sources and the consistency among them by unifying two regularization terms into our model. The proposed scheme naturally fits this application scenario.

Our main contributions can be summarized in twofold:

- We propose a novel MISTER model, which is able to model both the source confidence and source consistency. Specifically, we can obtain a closed-form solution by taking the inverse of a linear system, which has been mathematically proven to be invertible.

- We empirically evaluate our proposed scheme on the application of volunteerism tendency prediction. In addition, we develop a set of volunteer-oriented features to characterize users' volunteerism tendency. We have released our compiled dataset[1] to facilitate other researchers to repeat our experiments and verify their proposed approaches.

3.2   RELATED WORK

Our cross-discipline work is related to a broad spectrum of prior efforts, including volunteerism analysis, personality exploration, as well as multi-view learning with missing data.

3.2.1   VOLUNTEERISM AND PERSONALITY ANALYSIS

Volunteerism analysis has gained tremendous attention from scholars in social science in the past few years. The efforts mainly focus on exploring volunteering motivations and factors that affect volunteering decision [18, 28, 94, 119, 122]. Carlo et al. [18] demonstrated that personality traits, such as extraversion and agreeableness, are positively associated with volunteerism. Extraversion characterizes people who are talkative, active, and keen on socializing, while agreeableness characterizes people who are cooperative, helpful, and sympathetic to others [10]. Another study in [94] presented an advanced conceptual model of factors that contribute to the decision of volunteering. The proposed factors are *Demographic Characteristics*, *Personal Attributes*, *Volunteer Activators*, and *Social Pressure*. Recently, an ongoing project for implementing a volunteer-matching service was introduced in [47]. This project aims to match students' specialties as well as interests with the needs of the local nongovernmental organizations. It also enhances the "Town and Gown Relation" that exists between universities and the towns they reside in.

Additionally, as personality has been verified to be of high relevance to the volunteer behaviors [3, 20], we particularly explored the literature about personality prediction. The widely approved "Big Five" personality model was first systematically introduced in [80], which represents individual's personality at five broad dimensions: Extraversion, Agreeableness, Conscientiousness, Neuroticism, and Openness to Experience. Pennebaker et al. [92] analyzed the linguistic features for each personality trait and developed a transparent text analysis tool in psychology—Linguistic Inquiry and Word Count (LIWC). Moreover, many studies have been conducted to examine personality traits over various social media, including blogs [50, 126], social networks [8, 79, 98, 106], and even the community question and answer forums [11].

---

[1]The compiled dataset is publicly accessible via: http://multiplesocialnetworklearning.azurewebsites.net/.

In spite of the compelling success achieved by these social science researchers, far too little attention has been paid to identifying volunteers from social media. Moreover, most of the existing efforts [18, 94] employ surveys or face-to-face interviews with samples for data collection, which limits the scalability of their approaches. To bridge the gap, we propose this novel cross-discipline research, aiming to enhance social welfare by exploring the large-scale information in social media.

3.2.2 MULTI-VIEW LEARNING WITH MISSING DATA

Although our work is distinguished from multi-view learning, we can still benefit from their efforts. Zhang et al. [136] proposed an inductive multi-view multi-task learning model (reg-MVMT). regMVMT penalizes the disagreement of models learned from different sources over the unlabeled samples. The authors also studied the structured missing data, which is completely missing for a source in terms of a task. In other words, if a source is available for a task, then all samples will have data from this source. However, they overlooked the source weights and did not pay attention to the partially structured missing data, both of which are what we are concerned with. Yuan et al. [129] introduced an incomplete multi-source feature learning method, avoiding the direct inference of block-wise missing data. Particularly, the authors split the incomplete data into disjoint groups, where they conducted feature learning independently. However, such a mechanism constrains us to conduct source level analysis. Later, Xiang et al. [123] investigated multi-source learning with block-wise missing data with an application of Alzheimer's disease prediction and proposed the iSFS model. Apart from feature-level analysis, the authors also conducted source-level analysis by introducing the weights of models obtained from different sources. However, ignoring the consistency relationships among different models seems inappropriate. In addition, the authors also adapted the model to handle the cases where block-wise missing data exists. Different from their work, we infer the missing data by making full use of the available data before applying MISTER, which is more generalizable to other applications.

3.3 MULTIPLE SOCIAL NETWORK LEARNING

This section details our proposed MISTER model and derives its analytic solution by solving the inverse of a linear system, whose invertibility is proved rigorously.

3.3.1 NOTATION

Suppose we have a set of N labeled data samples and $S \geq 2$ social networks. We compile the S social networks with an index set $\mathcal{C} = \{1, 2, \cdots, S\}$. Let D_s and N_s denote the number of features and samples in the s-th social network, $s \in \mathcal{C}$, respectively. Let $\mathbf{X}_s \in \mathbb{R}^{N \times D_s}$ denote the feature matrix extracted from the s-th social network. Each row represents a user sample. Then the dimension of features extracted from all these social networks is $D = \sum_{s=1}^{S} D_s$. The whole feature matrix can be written as $\mathbf{X} = \{\mathbf{X}_1, \mathbf{X}_2, \cdots, \mathbf{X}_S\} \in \mathbb{R}^{N \times D}$ and $\mathbf{y} = \{y_1, y_2, \cdots, y_N\}^T \in \{1, -1\}^{N \times 1}$ is the corresponding label vector.

3.3.2 PROBLEM FORMULATIONS

Based on a set of data samples with S social networks, we can learn S predictive models, where each model is individually and independently trained on a social network. The final predictive model can be strengthened via linear combination of these S models. Mathematically, we learn one linear mapping function $\mathbf{f}_s$ for the s-th social network. In addition, we assume that the mapping functions learned from all social networks agree with one another as much as possible. Particularly, we can formalize this assumption using the regularization function. Using the least square loss function, we have the following objective function,

$$\min_{\mathbf{f}_s} \frac{1}{2N} \left\| \mathbf{y} - \mathbf{f}(\mathbf{X}) \right\|^2 + \frac{\mu}{2N} \sum_{s=1}^{S} \sum_{s' \neq s} \left\| \mathbf{f}_s(\mathbf{X}_s) - \mathbf{f}_{s'}(\mathbf{X}_{s'}) \right\|^2 + \frac{\lambda}{2} \left\| \mathbf{f} \right\|^2, \tag{3.1}$$

where $\mathbf{f}(\mathbf{X})$ is the final predictive model. $\mathbf{f}_s(\mathbf{X}_s)$ is the prediction result based upon data $\mathbf{X}_s$. λ and μ are the nonnegative regularization parameters that regulate the sparsity of the solution regarding $\mathbf{f}_s$ and the disagreement among models learned from different social networks, respectively. If we just treat the confidence of different social networks equally, the final predictive model can be formalized as follows,

$$\mathbf{f}(\mathbf{X}) = \frac{1}{S} \sum_{s=1}^{S} \mathbf{f}_s(\mathbf{X}_s). \tag{3.2}$$

However, in reality, different social networks always have different confidence to the final prediction, and we consider modeling the weights of multiple sources instead of treating all sources equally by introducing the weight vector: $\boldsymbol{\alpha} = [\alpha_1, \alpha_2, \cdots, \alpha_S]^T \in \mathbb{R}^{S \times 1}$, where α_s controls the weight of model learned from s-th social network. Then the final model is defined as follows,

$$\mathbf{f}(\mathbf{X}) = \sum_{s=1}^{S} \alpha_s \mathbf{f}_s(\mathbf{X}_s)$$
$$s.t. \quad \mathbf{e}^T \boldsymbol{\alpha} = 1, \tag{3.3}$$

where $\mathbf{e} = [1, 1, \cdots, 1]^T \in \mathbb{R}^{S \times 1}$. It is worth mentioning that we do not impose the constraint of $\alpha_s \geq 0$, as we want to keep both positive and negative weights. Positive weights indicate the positive correlations of social networks with the final results, while negative weights reflect negative correlations between the given task and different sources, which may contain unreliable and noisy data.

For the s-th social network, we learn a linear mapping function indexed by a model $\mathbf{w}_s \in \mathbb{R}^{D_s \times 1}$. Then the objective function can be rewritten as follows,

$$\min_{\mathbf{w}_s,\alpha} \frac{1}{2N} \left\| \mathbf{y} - \sum_{s=1}^{S} \alpha_s \mathbf{X}_s \mathbf{w}_s \right\|^2 + \frac{\mu}{2N} \sum_{s=1}^{S} \sum_{s' \neq s} \left\| \mathbf{X}_s \mathbf{w}_s - \mathbf{X}_{s'} \mathbf{w}_{s'} \right\|^2$$

$$+ \frac{\lambda}{2} \sum_{s=1}^{S} \left\| \mathbf{w}_s \right\|^2 + \frac{\beta}{2} \left\| \alpha \right\|^2 , \tag{3.4}$$

where $\mathbf{e}^T \alpha = 1$ and β is the regularization parameter, controlling the sparsity of the solution regarding α.

3.3.3 OPTIMIZATION

We adopt the alternating optimization strategy to solve the two variables α and $\mathbf{w}_s$ in Eq. (3.4). In particular, we optimize one variable while fixing the other one in each iteration. We keep this iterative procedure until the objective function converges.

Computing α with $\mathbf{w}_s$ Fixed

We denote the objective function as Γ. For simplicity, we replace $\mathbf{y}$ in Eq. (3.4) by $\mathbf{y}\mathbf{e}^T \alpha$, as $\mathbf{e}^T \alpha = 1$. With the help of Lagrangian, Γ can be rewritten as follows,

$$\min_{\alpha} \frac{1}{2N} \left\| \mathbf{y}\mathbf{e}^T \alpha - \mathbf{X}\mathbf{W}\alpha \right\|^2 + \frac{\beta}{2} \left\| \alpha \right\|^2 + \delta(1 - \mathbf{e}^T \alpha), \tag{3.5}$$

where δ is the nonnegative Lagrange multiplier and $\mathbf{W} = diag(\mathbf{w}_1, \mathbf{w}_2, \cdots, \mathbf{w}_S) \in \mathbb{R}^{D \times S}$. Taking derivative of Γ with respect to α, we have,

$$\frac{\partial \Gamma}{\partial \alpha} = \frac{1}{N} (\mathbf{y}\mathbf{e}^T - \mathbf{X}\mathbf{W})^T (\mathbf{y}\mathbf{e}^T - \mathbf{X}\mathbf{W})\alpha + \beta\alpha - \delta\mathbf{e}. \tag{3.6}$$

Setting Eq. (3.6) to zero, it can be derived that,

$$\alpha = \delta \mathbf{M}^{-1} \mathbf{e}, \tag{3.7}$$

where

$$\mathbf{M} = \frac{1}{N} (\mathbf{y}\mathbf{e}^T - \mathbf{X}\mathbf{W})^T (\mathbf{y}\mathbf{e}^T - \mathbf{X}\mathbf{W}) + \beta\mathbf{I}. \tag{3.8}$$

Since $\mathbf{e}^T \alpha = 1$, we can obtain that,

$$\delta = \frac{1}{\mathbf{e}^T \mathbf{M}^{-1} \mathbf{e}},$$

$$\alpha = \frac{\mathbf{M}^{-1} \mathbf{e}}{\mathbf{e}^T \mathbf{M}^{-1} \mathbf{e}}. \tag{3.9}$$

Obviously, $\mathbf{M} \in \mathbb{R}^{S \times S}$ is positive definite and invertible, according to the definition. We thus can obtain the analytic solution of $\boldsymbol{\alpha}$ as Eq. (3.9). Moreover, we note that when the prediction results learned from all social networks are equal, where $\mathbf{X}_1 \mathbf{w}_1 = \mathbf{X}_2 \mathbf{w}_2 = \cdots = \mathbf{X}_S \mathbf{w}_S$, then the same weights will be assigned, i.e., $\alpha_1 = \alpha_2 = \cdots = \alpha_S$. In addition, Eq. (3.9) tends to assign higher weight α_s, if smaller difference exists between $\mathbf{y}$ and $\mathbf{X}_s \mathbf{w}_s$.

Computing $\mathbf{w}_s$ with α Fixed

When $\boldsymbol{\alpha}$ is fixed, we compute the derivative of $\boldsymbol{\Gamma}$ regarding $\mathbf{w}_s$ as follows,

$$
\begin{aligned}
\frac{\partial \boldsymbol{\Gamma}}{\partial \mathbf{w}_s} &= \frac{1}{N} \alpha_s \mathbf{X}_s^T \left(\sum_{s=1}^{S} \alpha_s \mathbf{X}_s \mathbf{w}_s - \mathbf{y} \right) \\
&\quad + \frac{\mu}{N} \mathbf{X}_s^T \sum_{s' \neq s} (\mathbf{X}_s \mathbf{w}_s - \mathbf{X}_{s'} \mathbf{w}_{s'}) + \lambda \mathbf{w}_s \\
&= \left[\lambda \mathbf{I} + \frac{\alpha_s^2}{N} \mathbf{X}_s^T \mathbf{X}_s + \frac{\mu(S-1)}{N} \mathbf{X}_s^T \mathbf{X}_s \right] \mathbf{w}_s \\
&\quad + \sum_{s' \neq s} \frac{1}{N} (\alpha_s \alpha_{s'} - \mu) \mathbf{X}_s^T \mathbf{X}_{s'} \mathbf{w}_{s'} - \frac{\alpha_s}{N} \mathbf{X}_s^T \mathbf{y},
\end{aligned}
\tag{3.10}
$$

where $\mathbf{I}$ is a $D_s \times D_s$ identity matrix. Setting Eq. (3.10) to zero and rearranging the terms, all $\mathbf{w}_s$'s can be learned jointly by the following linear system,

$$
\mathbf{L} \mathbf{w} = \mathbf{t}
$$

$$
\begin{bmatrix}
\mathbf{L}_{11} & \mathbf{L}_{12} & \mathbf{L}_{13} & \cdots & \mathbf{L}_{1S} \\
\mathbf{L}_{21} & \mathbf{L}_{22} & \mathbf{L}_{23} & \cdots & \mathbf{L}_{2S} \\
\mathbf{L}_{31} & \mathbf{L}_{32} & \mathbf{L}_{33} & \cdots & \mathbf{L}_{3S} \\
\vdots & \vdots & \vdots & \ddots & \vdots \\
\mathbf{L}_{S1} & \mathbf{L}_{S2} & \mathbf{L}_{S3} & \cdots & \mathbf{L}_{SS}
\end{bmatrix}
\begin{bmatrix}
\mathbf{w}_1 \\
\mathbf{w}_2 \\
\mathbf{w}_3 \\
\vdots \\
\mathbf{w}_S
\end{bmatrix}
=
\begin{bmatrix}
\mathbf{t}_1 \\
\mathbf{t}_2 \\
\mathbf{t}_3 \\
\vdots \\
\mathbf{t}_S
\end{bmatrix},
\tag{3.11}
$$

where $\mathbf{L} \in \mathbb{R}^{D \times D}$ is a sparse block matrix with $S \times S$ blocks, $\mathbf{w} = [\mathbf{w}_1^T, \mathbf{w}_2^T, \cdots, \mathbf{w}_S^T]^T \in \mathbb{R}^{D \times 1}$ and $\mathbf{t} = [\mathbf{t}_1^T, \mathbf{t}_2^T, \cdots, \mathbf{t}_S^T]^T \in \mathbb{R}^{D \times 1}$ are both sparse block vectors with $S \times 1$ blocks. $\mathbf{t}_s$, $\mathbf{L}_{ss}$ and $\mathbf{L}_{ss'}$ are defined as follows,

$$
\begin{cases}
\mathbf{t}_s &= \frac{\alpha_s}{N} \mathbf{X}_s^T \mathbf{y}, \\
\mathbf{L}_{ss} &= \lambda \mathbf{I} + \frac{\alpha_s^2 - \mu}{N} \mathbf{X}_s^T \mathbf{X}_s + \frac{\mu S}{N} \mathbf{X}_s^T \mathbf{X}_s, \\
\mathbf{L}_{ss'} &= \frac{\alpha_s \alpha_{s'} - \mu}{N} \mathbf{X}_s^T \mathbf{X}_{s'}.
\end{cases}
\tag{3.12}
$$

Technically, $\mathbf{t}$ can be treated as a constant matrix as $\boldsymbol{\alpha}$ is fixed. It is worth noting that $\mathbf{L}$ is symmetric as $\mathbf{L}_{ss'} = \mathbf{L}_{s's}^T$. If we can prove that $\mathbf{L}$ is invertible, then we can derive the closed-form solution of $\mathbf{w}$ as follows,

$$
\mathbf{w} = \mathbf{L}^{-1} \mathbf{t}.
\tag{3.13}
$$

We now show $\mathbf{L}$ is invertible by proving that $\mathbf{L}$ is a positive-definite matrix. Let $\mathbf{h} = [\mathbf{h}_1^T, \mathbf{h}_2^T, \cdots, \mathbf{h}_S^T]^T \in \mathbb{R}^{D \times 1} \neq \mathbf{0}$ be an arbitrary block vector, where $\mathbf{h}_i \in \mathbb{R}^{D_i \times 1}, i \in \mathcal{C}$. Then we need to prove that $\mathbf{h}^T \mathbf{L} \mathbf{h}$

$$= \sum_{i=1}^{S} \sum_{j=1}^{S} \mathbf{h}_i^T \mathbf{L}_{ij} \mathbf{h}_j$$

$$= \lambda \|\mathbf{h}\|^2 + \frac{1}{N} \Big[\sum_{i=1}^{S} \|\alpha_i \mathbf{X}_i \mathbf{h}_i\|^2 + \mu(S-1) \sum_{i=1}^{S} \|\mathbf{X}_i \mathbf{h}_i\|^2$$

$$+ \sum_{i=1}^{S} \sum_{j \neq i} \alpha_i \mathbf{h}_i^T \mathbf{X}_i^T \alpha_j \mathbf{X}_j \mathbf{h}_j - \mu \sum_{i=1}^{S} \sum_{j \neq i} \mathbf{h}_i^T \mathbf{X}_i^T \mathbf{X}_j \mathbf{h}_j \Big], \tag{3.14}$$

is always larger than zero. In fact, given an arbitrary vector $\mathbf{b}_i$, we have,

$$\sum_{i=1}^{S} \sum_{j \neq i} \|\mathbf{b}_i - \mathbf{b}_j\|^2 \geq 0$$

$$(S-1) \sum_{i=1}^{S} \|\mathbf{b}_i\|^2 \geq \sum_{i=1}^{S} \sum_{j \neq i} \mathbf{b}_i^T \mathbf{b}_j. \tag{3.15}$$

Therefore, we have the following inequality,

$$\mu(S-1) \sum_{i=1}^{S} \|\mathbf{X}_i \mathbf{h}_i\|^2 \geq \mu \sum_{i=1}^{S} \sum_{j \neq i} (\mathbf{X}_i \mathbf{h}_i)^T \mathbf{X}_j \mathbf{h}_j. \tag{3.16}$$

Besides, we know that,

$$\sum_{i=1}^{S} \|\alpha_i \mathbf{X}_i \mathbf{h}_i\|^2 + \sum_{i=1}^{S} \sum_{j \neq i} \alpha_i \mathbf{h}_i^T \mathbf{X}_i^T \alpha_j \mathbf{X}_j \mathbf{h}_j = \Big\| \sum_{i=1}^{S} \alpha_i \mathbf{X}_i \mathbf{h}_i \Big\|^2 \geq 0. \tag{3.17}$$

Based upon Eq. (3.16) and Eq. (3.17), we have that,

$$\mathbf{h}^T \mathbf{L} \mathbf{h} \geq \lambda \|\mathbf{h}\|^2. \tag{3.18}$$

As $\mathbf{h} \neq \mathbf{0}$, $\mathbf{h}^T \mathbf{L} \mathbf{h}$ is always larger than zero. Consequently, $\mathbf{L}$ is invertible. The overall procedures for alternating optimization are summarized in Algorithm 2. As each iteration can decrease Γ, whose lower bound is zero, we can guarantee the convergence of Algorithm 2 [37, 86].

3.4   EXPERIMENTATION

We verified our proposed model from various angles on the application of volunteerism tendency prediction. Extensive experiments were conducted over a system equipped with Intel i7 2.60 GHz CPU, and 8 GB memory. In particular, we launched 10-fold cross validation for each experiment, and reported the average performance. Each fold involves 2,249 training and 250 testing samples.

Algorithm 2 Alternative optimization for solving Eq. (3.4)

Input: $\mathbf{X}, \mathbf{y}, \lambda, \beta, \mu$

Output: $\alpha, \mathbf{w}$

1: Initialize $(\mathbf{w})^0$ by fitting each source individually on the available data. Initialize $(\alpha)^0 = [\frac{1}{S}, \frac{1}{S}, \cdots, \frac{1}{S}]$.

2: **for** $k = 1, 2, \cdots$ **do**

3:    Compute each $(\alpha)^k$ according to Eq. (3.9).

4:    Update $(\mathbf{w})^k$ according to Eq. (3.13).

5:    **if** the objective value stops decreasing **then**

6:        return $\alpha = (\alpha)^k$ and $\mathbf{w} = (\mathbf{w})^k$

7:    **end if**

8: **end for**

3.4.1   EXPERIMENTAL SETTINGS

Data Collection

We proposed two strategies to collect data from About.me.

- **Keyword search**: We searched About.me with the keyword "volunteer" and obtained 4,151 volunteer candidates.

- **Random select**: We employed Random API,[2] provided by About.me, to collect non-volunteers candidates. This API returns a specified number of random user profiles. Finally, we harvested 1,867 non-volunteer candidates. It is worth mentioning that volunteers may be present in these random users.

To enlarge our dataset, we also collected candidates from Quora by the breadth-first-search method. Particularly, we took advantage of both the follower and followee[3] relations provided by Quora. Initially, we selected two popular users as the seed users and then explored all their neighboring connected users. We applied similar exploration approach to all other non-seed users. In the end, we collected 172,235 users' profiles and only retained those who have accounts in Facebook, Twitter, and LinkedIn.

Based on these candidates, we launched a crawler to collect their historical social content, including their basic profiles, social posts, and relations. However, the traditional web-based crawler is not applicable to Facebook due to its dynamic loading mechanism. We thus resorted to the Selenium[4] to simulate users' click and scroll operations on a FireFox browser and load users' publicly available information. We limited the access rate to one request per second to avoid being blocked by the robot checkers. It is worth mentioning that the data we collected is all publicly

---

[2]http://about.me/developer/api/docs/
[3]If A follows B, then A is B's follower and B is A's followee.
[4]http://docs.seleniumhq.org/download/

available. On the other hand, due to the privacy constraint, we could not access users' social relations in Facebook and LinkedIn. We hence only collected users' followee relations in Twitter.

Ground Truth Construction

In order to improve the quality of our dataset, we employed three annotators to finalize our ground truth. As users tend to provide more complete and reliable profiles in LinkedIn, we guided the annotators to study the LinkedIn profiles of candidate users, and determine whether they are "volunteers" by majority votes. To ensure a uniformly labeling procedure, we provided them a guideline. Given a user's LinkedIn profile, we classified a user as a volunteer if and only if this user lists his/her volunteer experiences in the section "Volunteer experience & Causes" or "Experience." Candidates who do not satisfy the above two criteria were tagged as non-volunteers. We focused on LinkedIn to determine whether users are volunteers because the volunteer experiences on LinkedIn are the most straightforward evidence to identify volunteers. It should be noted that those who do not mention their volunteer experiences on LinkedIn are not necessarily classified as "non-volunteers." However, the absence of these mentions, at least, reveals their limited interests and low enthusiasm in volunteerism. Therefore, in our work, we broadly defined users as "non-volunteers" if they do not mention their relevant volunteerism experiences on LinkedIn.

Table 3.1 lists the statistics of our dataset. We obtained the data for 1,425 volunteers and 4,011 non-volunteers according to the aforementioned strategies. The crawling was conducted between August 22 and September 11, 2013. Here we only selected a subset of non-volunteer data and made the dataset balanced to avoid the training bias. To facilitate this line of research, this dataset was released after certain privacy preservation processing.

Table 3.1: Statistics of our collected dataset from multiple social networks

Data	Volunteer	Non-volunteer
Twitter profiles	~1.5 k	~4 k
Twitter posts	~559 k	~1 m
Twitter followees' profiles	~902 k	~3 m
Facebook profiles	~1.5 k	~4 k
Facebook posts	~83 k	~228 k
LinkedIn profiles	~1.5 k	~4 k

3.4.2 FEATURE EXTRACTION

To capture users' volunteerism tendency, we extracted a rich set of volunteer-oriented features, comprising demographic, linguistic, and behavior features.

Demographic Characteristics

The study in [94] reported that some demographic characteristics, such as education and income level, are strong indicators for volunteerism. This study inspires us to extract demographic characteristics from users' profiles, especially the Facebook and LinkedIn profiles. In our work, we explored users' demographic characteristics, including *Gender*, *Relationship status*, *Education level*, and *Number of social connections*.

Linguistic Features

We also extracted linguistic features, including Linguistic Inquiry and Word Count (LIWC) features, user topics, and contextual topics:

- **LIWC features.** LIWC is widely used to analyze the psycho-linguistic transparent lexicon. It plays an important role in predicting users' personality [11, 79]. The main component of LIWC is a directory which contains the mapping from words to 72 categories.[5] Given a document, LIWC computes the percentage of words in each category and represents it as a vector of 72 dimensions. To capture the key aspects of LIWC features, we selected the top 5 dimensions as the representative LIWC features according to the information gain ratio. Considering that emotions may also affect users' volunteerism tendency, we additionally selected two categories from LIWC: positive emotion and negative emotion. We also utilized the positive-negative emotion ratio to further reflect users' emotional states. Let $L(\bullet)$ represent the percentage of users' words in certain LIWC category. The positive-negative emotion ratio is defined as,

$$PN_{emo} = L(pos)log\frac{L(pos) + \xi_p}{L(neg) + \xi_n},\qquad(3.19)$$

  where ξ_p and ξ_n are introduced to avoid the situation: individuals have no positive or negative emotional word. They are both set as 0.0001. In total, we have 16 dimension LIWC features, extracted from Twitter and Facebook.

- **User topics.** According to our observation, volunteers may have, on average, a higher probability of talking about topics such as social caring or giving back, while the non-volunteers may mention other topics more often. This motivates us to explore the topic distributions of users' social posts to identify volunteers. We generated topic distributions using Latent Dirichlet Allocation (LDA) [15], which has been widely found to be useful in latent topic modeling [43, 120]. Based on the perplexity [69] metric frequently utilized to find the optimal number of hidden topics, we ultimately obtained 52, 26, 42 dimensional topic-level features over users' Twitter, Facebook, and LinkedIn data, respectively.

- **Contextual topics.** We define users' contextual topics as the topics of users' connections. We believe that the contextual topics intuitively reflect the contexts of users. "He that lies

---

[5]http://www.liwc.net/

down with dogs must rise up with fleas" tells us that the context significantly affects a user's tendency. Particularly, we studied followees and retweeting[6] connections on Twitter because of their intuitive reflection of topics that concern users. As the bio descriptions are usually provided by users to briefly introduce themselves and may indicate users' summarized interests, we integrated the bios of a user's followees or those whose tweets are retweeted by this user into two kinds of bio documents, on which we further applied LDA model. We utilized the perplexity to fix the dimensions of topic-level features over followees' bio documents and retweetings' bio documents as 40 and 20, respectively. In this work, we only explored the contextual topics on Twitter, since we were unable to crawl the connections' profiles on LinkedIn and the bio descriptions are usually missing on Facebook.

Behavior-based features

This kind of feature is characterized by users' posting behavior patterns and networking behavior patterns. The former focuses on the written style of users' social posts, while the latter captures their egocentric network features:

- **Posting behavior patterns.** Posting behavior patterns have been investigated in many scenarios, spanning from age estimation to social spammers discovery [12, 66]. These patterns can be used to depict users' participation in information diffusion, which correlates with volunteerism tendency much. On one hand, we employed the fraction of users' posts containing certain behaviors, including emoticons, slang words, acronyms, hashtags, URLs, and user mentions, to intuitively reflect users' engagement in topic discussion and social interaction. On the other hand, we observed that users' posting behaviors on social networks can be classified into a few categories. For example, posts on Twitter can be classified into two categories, $C_{tw} = \{tweets, retweets\}$, while posts on Facebook can be roughly split into eight types: $C_{fb} = \{share\_link, share\_sideo, share\_status, share\_photo, change\_pho, repost, post, tagged\}$. The distributions over users' posts on these categories also reflect their participation in information diffusion, revealing whether a given user tends to share information in social networks. When it comes to Linkedin, we utilized the profile completeness to characterize users' behaviors. Based on our observation, we found that volunteers tend to provide more information for all the sections. This not only reflects volunteers' active participation in LinkedIn but also signals their self-confidence and openness to public. Profile completeness is defined as a boolean vector over six dimensions to denote the presence of the six common sections in LinkedIn profiles: `summary`, `interest`, `language`, `education`, `skill`, and `honor`. We excluded the sections on `experience` and `volunteer experience & causes`, because the ground truth is built on these two sections.

---

[6]If A broadcasts a tweet posted by B, then B is A's retweeting user.

- **Egocentric network patterns.** We also studied users' social behaviors from their egocentric networks. Intuitively, we believe that users who belong to certain class tend to be connected with several class-specific accounts ("birds of a feather flock together"). Therefore, volunteers should interact with some typical accounts on social media. The set of typical accounts is denoted as FV. Inspired by [90], we measured the degree of a user's correlation with volunteerism by three features: the frequency and fraction of a user's "friends" that belong to FV as well as the total number of "friends." In particular, we treated both the followees and retweetings as the "friends" of users on Twitter. To construct the FV, we utilized the Twitter profile repository Wefollow,[7] which allows us to find the most prominent people given a particular category. By crawling prominent users falling into categories of *Nonprofit*, *Charity*, *Volunteer*, *NGO*, *Community Service*, *Social Welfare*, and *Christian* from Wefollow, we obtained 23,285 accounts.

3.4.3 MODEL COMPARISON

We compared MISTER with four baselines. Before that, the data was completed by MSNDC. We also performed significant tests to validate the effectiveness of MISTER.

- SVM: We chose the learning formulation with the kernel of radial-basis function. We implemented this method based on LIBSVM [21].

- RLS: Regularized least squares model [59] aims to minimize the objective function of $\frac{1}{2N} \|\mathbf{y} - \mathbf{Xw}\|^2 + \frac{\lambda}{2} \|\mathbf{w}\|^2$. In fact, the RLS model can be deduced from MISTER via the settings of $\alpha = [\frac{1}{S}, \frac{1}{S}, \cdots, \frac{1}{S}]^T$, $\mu = 0$ and $\beta = 0$.

- iSFS: The third baseline is the incomplete source-feature selection model proposed in [123]. This model only assigns weights to models learned from different social networks but ignores the relationships among them. We can derive iSFS from MISTER by making $\mu = 0$.

- regMVMT: The fourth baseline is the regularized multi-view multi-task learning model [136]. This model only regulates the relationships among different views but fails to take the source confidence into account. We can derive regMVMT from MISTER by making $\alpha = [\frac{1}{S}, \frac{1}{S}, \cdots, \frac{1}{S}]^T$.

Table 3.2 shows the performance comparison between baselines and our proposed MISTER. We noticed that MISTER significantly outperforms the SVM and RLS. This implies that the information on multiple social networks are complementary and characterize users' volunteerism tendency consistently. This also proves that the correlations of different social networks with the task of volunteerism tendency prediction cannot be treated equally. In addition, MISTER achieves better performance, as compared with iSFS and regMVMT, which are the derivations of MISTER. This demonstrates that both the source confidence and the source consistency deserve particular attention.

---

[7]http://wefollow.com/

Table 3.2: Performance comparison among different models for volunteerism tendency prediction. P-values denote the pairwise significance test results between our model and each of the competitors.

Approaches	F1-measure	P-value
SVM	83.11	0.038
RLS	82.82	0.025
regMVMT	84.07	0.173
iSFS	84.72	0.281
MISTER	**85.59**	–

3.4.4 DATA COMPLETION COMPARISON

We further evaluated the component for missing data completion with the following three baseline methods.

- Remove: This method eliminates all data samples that are not complete.

- Average: This method imputes the missing features with the average values of the corresponding feature items.

- KNN: The missing data is inferred by averaging its K-nearest neighbors. K is experimentally set as 1.

Table 3.3 shows the performance of different models over different data completion strategies. It can be seen that MSNDC outperforms the other strategies. Additionally, removing all incomplete data samples achieves the worst performance, which may be caused by the fact that it introduces training bias, making the dataset unbalanced and reduces the size of training dataset. We found that the percentage of volunteer samples decreases from 50% to 40% after filtering out all incomplete data samples.

Table 3.3: Performance of different models over different data completion strategies

Approaches	SVM	RLS	MISTER
Remove	74.91	74.66	81.81
Average	82.09	81.99	85.43
KNN	82.60	82.22	85.55
MSNDC	83.11	82.82	**85.59**

3.4.5   FEATURE COMPARISON

To examine the discriminative features we extracted, we conducted experiments over different kinds of features using MISTER. We also performed a significant test to validate the advantage of combining multiple social networks. Table 3.4 comparatively shows the performance of MISTER in terms of different feature configurations. It can be seen that the linguistic features achieves the best performance, as compared against demographic characteristics and behavior-based features. This reveals that a volunteerism tendency is better reflected by their social content, including their own social posts and the self-descriptions of their social connections. This also implies that users with a volunteerism tendency may talk about related topics and follow or retweet related social accounts. In addition, we found that contextual topics are more discriminative as compared to users' own topics. This may be due to the fact that users' self-descriptions are of more value and contain less noise than users' tweets. Some hot topics discussed by volunteers are given in Table 3.5. The egocentric network patterns also play a dominant role in our task. This implies that one's social connections indeed reflect the user's personal concerns to a large extent.

Table 3.4: Performance of our proposed model over different feature combinations (%)

Features	F1-measure
Demographic characteristics	**68.43**
Linquistic features	**80.06**
User topics	75.04
Contextual topics	78.14
LIWC	68.48
Behavior-based features	**78.52**
Posting behavior patterns	69.83
Egocentric network patterns	75.91

3.4.6   SOURCE COMPARISON

To demonstrate the descriptiveness of multiple social network integration, we conducted experiments over various source combinations. Notably, data from Facebook and LinkedIn is incomplete and we need to infer the block-wise missing data first taking advantage of the complete data samples from Twitter.

Table 3.6 shows the performance of MISTER over different social network combinations. We noted that the more sources we incorporate, the better the performance can be achieved. This implies the complementary relationships rather than mutual conflicting relationships among the sources. Moreover, we found that aggregating data from all these three social networks can achieve significantly better performance as compared to each of the single sources. Additionally,

Table 3.5: Hot topics discussed by volunteers. Contextual topics are generated from followee and retweeting. User topics are generated from their own profiles.

Data source	Topic Words
Followee	• public, politics, rights, development
	• editor, global, journalist, university
Retweeting	• global, nonprofit, change, community
	• health, education, learning, university
Self	• woman, help, education, child
	• volunteer, nonprofit, support

Table 3.6: Performance of our proposed model over different social network combinations(%). Facebook∗ and LinkedIn∗ both refer to the complete data, whose missing data is pre-inferred. F1: F1-measure.

Social Network Combinations	F1	P-value
Twitter	82.35	4.2e-2
Facebook*	73.53	5.0e-7
LinkedIn*	74.49	3.1e-7
Twitter + Facebook*	83.67	1.1e-1
Twitter + LinkedIn*	83.84	1.4e-1
Facebook* + LinkedIn*	76.29	6.0e-6
Twitter + Facebook* + LinkedIn*	**85.59**	–

as the performances obtained from different single social networks are not the same, this validates that incorporating the confidence of different social networks to MISTER is reasonable. Interestingly, we observed that MISTER over Twitter alone achieves the much better performance, as compared to that over LinkedIn or Facebook alone. This may be caused by the fact that the most discriminative features evaluated by Section 3.4.5 are all extracted from Twitter.

3.4.7   SIZE VARYING OF POSITIVE SAMPLES

In order to verify the usefulness of our model on a real world dataset, where the volunteers should account for a minority portion of a user population, we tuned the fraction of volunteer samples in our dataset. In particular, we fed x%, $x \in [5, 50]$, of volunteer samples to our model with stepsize 5%. Figure 3.2 shows the F1-measure with respect to different fractions of volunteer samples of different models. As can be seen, our model can achieve satisfactory performance even when volunteer samples only account for 5% of the whole samples. This demonstrates that the proposed

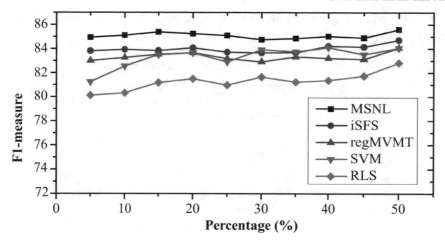

Figure 3.2: The performance of various models in terms of F1-measure. The size of training samples varies.

MISTER model is not sensitive to the percentage of positive samples. Whereas, SVM and RLS are relatively more sensitive to the fraction of volunteer samples in dataset.

3.4.8 COMPLEXITY DISCUSSION

In order to analyze the complexity of MISTER, we need to solve the time complexity in terms of constructing $\mathbf{M}$, $\mathbf{L}$, and $\mathbf{t}$ as defined in Eq. (3.8) and Eq. (3.12), and computing the inverse of $\mathbf{M}$ and $\mathbf{L}$. Assuming $D \gg S$, the construction of matrix $\mathbf{M}$ has a time complexity of $\mathbf{O}(NDS)$, and the construction of matrix $\mathbf{L}$ has a time complexity of $\mathbf{O}(ND^2)$. Due to the fact that the cost of matrix multiplications $(\mathbf{X}_s^T \mathbf{X}_{s'})$ and that of constructing $\mathbf{t}$ involved in Eq. (3.12) remain the same for all iterations and $\mathbf{L}$ is symmetric, we can save much practical time cost. Also, using the standard method, computing the inverse of two core matrices, $\mathbf{M}$ and $\mathbf{L}$, has the complexity of $\mathbf{O}(S^3)$ and $\mathbf{O}(D^3)$, respectively. Furthermore, using the method of Coppersmith and Winogard, the time cost can be bounded by $\mathbf{O}(S^{2.376})$ and $\mathbf{O}(D^{2.376})$ [134], respectively. We note that the speed bottleneck lies in the number of features and the number of social networks instead of the number of data samples. As S and D are usually small, especially S, MISTER should be efficient in time complexity.

To validate the practical efficiency of the proposed MISTER model, we conducted a set of experiments. The comparison of average time consumption of different models is shown in Table 3.7. As can be seen, MISTER shows superiority over SVM in terms of the time cost, which takes only 19% of the time that SVM uses. By careful observation, we observed that MISTER converges very quickly, which on average takes about 20 iterations. Even though MISTER takes more time than RLS and regMVMT due to the consideration of source consistency and source confidence, it improves the performance in terms of F1-measure.

Table 3.7: Comparative illustration of time cost among different models (%)

Approaches	Total(s)	Train(s)	Test(s)
SVM	2.0550	1.8211	0.2339
RLS	0.0639	0.0631	0.0008
regMVMT	0.0605	0.0595	0.0006
iSFS	0.5565	0.5557	0.0008
MISTER	0.3936	0.3929	0.0007

3.5   SUMMARY

In this chapter, we presented a novel scheme for multi-source mono-task learning. We argued that the views revealed by different social networks may vary according to the different services they offer, which are complimentary to each other and comprehensively characterize a specific user from different perspectives. As compared to the scarce knowledge conveyed by a single source, appropriate aggregation of multiple social networks offers us a better opportunity for deep user understanding. We hence jointly take the source confidence and source consistency into consideration by introducing regularization to the objective function. We practically evaluated the proposed scheme in an interesting scenario of volunteerism tendency prediction. We developed a set of volunteer-oriented features to characterize users' volunteerism tendency. Extensive experimental results have demonstrated the effectiveness of our proposed scheme and verified the advantages of utilizing multiple social networks over a single source. The proposed scheme is applicable to many other binary classification applications, such as gender inference and item recommendation.

CHAPTER 4

Mono-source Multi-task Learning

4.1 APPLICATION: USER INTEREST INFERENCE FROM MONO-SOURCE

Beyond multi-source mono-task learning as introduced in Chapter 3, this chapter presents the mono-source multi-task learning model and its application in user interest inference. User interest inference is the basis for many applications. Cold-start problems [104], adaptive E-learning [109], computational target advertisement [32], and personalized services [62] all benefit from a detailed knowledge of the interests of the user in order to personalize the results and improve relevance. Take target advertisements as an example. Users' online behaviors on the prominent social platforms, such as Twitter, Quora, and Facebook, are mostly interest-driven, which essentially reflect users' personal preferences and interests. This makes it feasible to infer user interest from social media.

Despite the importance and feasibility of user interest mining, it poses a unique set of challenges that make it difficult to directly borrow techniques from earlier efforts. The challenges include: (a) **Label Variants**. Users are encouraged to explicitly list their interests on some social sites, such as LinkedIn, which saves our labeling efforts. However, due to their diverse educational and linguistic backgrounds, users frequently describe the same interest using different concepts. For instance, two users have the same interest in "programming," but they may use two different terms—"web development" and "coding"—to describe their interests. This leads to the problem of limited training samples. Usually, multi-task learning assigns each interest with one task. We hence should group these variant concepts into the same cluster and reinforce the inference performance by learning the related multiple tasks simultaneously. (b) **Interest Relatedness**. Interests are usually not independent but correlated to each other in a non-uniform and complex way. We have to automatically establish a structure to capture the inherent relatedness of the pairwise interests. (c) **Grouping Structure**. The grouping of interests depends on users' social context, instead of just the similarities between the interest concepts. For instance, "golf" and "investment" are the interests frequently preferred by the same persons; while "golf" and "football" are less likely to be associated even though they are related as sports. Hence, the taxonomic prior knowledge of interest concepts cannot accurately reflect the true grouping structure. It is thus necessary to discover the underlying grouping structure of interests based on users' historical posts.

To address the aforementioned problems, we propose a novel model, named eFficient cLustered mUlti-Task lEarning (FLUTE), which treats each interest as a task. It is able to automatically learn a sophisticated grouping structure of the tasks, without even the need to pre-specify the number of clusters. Based upon this structure, FLUTE co-regularizes the following factors to maximize the knowledge sharing among multiple related tasks: (a) **Global relatedness**. All the task pairs share information to some extent, including the tasks in different groups. But their strengthens vary, and FLUTE is able to characterize and model such global relatedness. (b) **Intra-relatedness**. Tasks within the same group are enforced to be similar. (c) **Inter-relatedness**. Close similarities between tasks from different groups are penalized. We have theoretically demonstrated the analytical solution of this model. To further boost the learning performance, we leverage the solutions of the desired tasks to adjust the grouping structure, and the refined structure in turn tunes the solution. Different from traditional clustered multi-task learning (CMTL), we have only one layer iteration and in practice, it converges very fast.

In summary:

- We proposed a novel and efficient clustered multi-task learning model, which automatically organizes tasks into a graph structure and groups the tasks into various clusters. Meanwhile, we incorporated the modularity function to discover the optimal grouping structure.

- We theoretically demonstrated the closed-form solution for the desired tasks, rather than gradient descent solutions. This ensures that our model can be solved efficiently.

- Most importantly, we have released the code, parameter settings, and data to facilitate other researchers to reproduce our experiments and verify their own models.[1]

4.2   RELATED WORK

4.2.1   CLUSTERED MULTI-TASK LEARNING

Recent years have witnessed that multi-task learning (MTL) has been an active and growing area of interest in machine learning [137, 143]. MTL is the idea of pooling related tasks together in a joint analysis. Previous empirical work has shown that combining tasks in a predictor model can achieve better generalization performance than learning each task separately, especially with the conditions where there are insufficient training samples [74]. The key issue in MTL is how to characterize and model the relatedness among tasks. A wide variety of MTL approaches have been developed based on a large range of the dependence structure among tasks, such as the uniform relatedness between pairwise tasks [139], tree-guided relatedness among tasks [45, 60], graph-regularized relatedness among tasks [4, 107], as well as the higher-order task relationships [140]. Most of the above methods were designed by assuming some fixed and prior known structures shared by all the tasks. However, such task structures may not be available in many real cases and the "right" latent task structures should be learned in a data-driven manner. This motivates the

---

[1]https://FLUTE.farbox.com

development of CMTL, which assumes that the tasks can be partitioned into a set of groups where the tasks within the same groups are much closer to each other than those from different groups, and such underlying grouping structure is unknown as a priori that needs to be learned from the data. An advantage of these approaches is their robustness against outlier tasks because they reside in separate clusters that do not affect other tasks. It is worth mentioning that there have been many prior efforts along the research line of CMTL, such as the models presented in [53, 145]. These research achievements have been successfully applied to many applications, ranging from object detection in computer vision [130] to community detection in social networks [111]. Despite its significant value, existing CMTL approaches still suffer from three limitations. First, they need to pre-specify the number of clusters for the underlying grouping structures; however, this is rarely known a priori in real-world situations. Second, the solutions to these existing models often exhibit two layer iterations, rather than closed-form solutions, which greatly hinder their efficiencies. Third, existing approaches frequently overlook the weak relatedness between tasks that are in different clusters, which may cause information loss. Our proposed model can address these difficult problems.

4.2.2 USER INTEREST MINING

With the rising popularity of social media, mining user interests has attracted so much attention [25, 44, 71, 118]. Broadly speaking, existing efforts on user interest mining from social media can be classified into two categories from the machine learning angle. One is individual task learning [13, 118, 128, 128]. For instance, the authors in [13] observed that users on Twitter generally follow experts on various topics of their interests in order to acquire information on those topics. A shallow learning method based on social annotations was employed first to deduce the topical expertise of popular Twitter users, and then transitively infer the interests of the users who follow them. Another work was introduced in [87], in which the authors viewed users' actions as a resource to express their interests, such as tweeting on Twitter, reblogging on Tumblr, and liking on Facebook. A rich set of features were then extracted to represent these actions and various models such as SVM were trained to predict the interests of users. In the context of individual task learning, the prediction function of each interest task is learned separately and the correlations among tasks are not explored. The other line of effort is multi-task learning. They take the task relatedness into account to boost the learning performance and alleviate the problem of insufficient training samples that the traditional individual task learning is facing [36]. Most recently, Song et al. [113] proposed an interest mining model via structure-constrained multi-task learning, where the tasks were pre-organized into a tree structure based upon the internal and external knowledge, respectively. However, the multi-task learning models designed for interest mining from social media either did not consider the structures among interests, or need the structures before learning. As an improved work, our proposed model automatically learns the underlying hidden structures to represent the relatedness among tasks and uses such structures to reinforce the multi-task learning.

4.3 EFFICIENT CLUSTERED MULTI-TASK LEARNING

4.3.1 NOTATION

Suppose we are given a set of N labeled samples and T tasks. Let's use $\mathbf{Y} = [\mathbf{y}_1, \mathbf{y}_2, \ldots, \mathbf{y}_T] \in \mathbb{R}^{N \times T}$ and $\mathbf{X} \in \mathbb{R}^{N \times D}$ to respectively denote the label vector and the extracted feature matrix of these N samples, where D represents the feature dimension.

In this work, we assume that there exists a hidden graph, $\mathbf{G}$, over the given dataset, where each vertex denotes a task and the edge weight between two tasks reflects their pairwise related-ness. We use an adjacent matrix $\mathbf{A}$ to represent such graph and its (i, j)-th entry A_{ij}, to denote the nonnegative relatedness between the i-th and j-th tasks. To discover the hidden grouping struc-ture among tasks, we partition $\mathbf{G}$ into subgraphs $\mathbf{G}$. For a given subgraph $\mathbf{G}_c$ in $\mathbf{G}$, its support set of vertices is denoted as $\sigma(\mathbf{c})$.[2] $|\sigma(\mathbf{c})|$ denotes the number of tasks in $\mathbf{G}_c$ with a probabilistic index vector $\mathbf{c} = [c_1, c_2, \ldots, c_T]^T$, where the component $c_i = \frac{1}{|\sigma(\mathbf{c})|}$ if the i-th task belongs to $\mathbf{G}_c$, otherwise $c_i = 0$. We can see that c_i means the probability of the i-th task falling into this group.

For each graph, we can find its optimal partition based upon the given metric. Let's denote such partition with a probabilistic index matrix $\mathbf{M} = [\mathbf{c}^1, \mathbf{c}^2, \ldots, \mathbf{c}^K]$, which indicates the parti-tion of all tasks over K groups. It is worth mentioning that in our work each task is forced to asso-ciate with only one group and hence the columns in $\mathbf{M}$ are orthogonal, i.e., $\mathbf{c}^{i^T} \mathbf{c}^j = 0, \forall i \neq j$.

4.3.2 PROBLEM FORMULATION

Our research objective is to automatically discover the optimal hidden graph from the given data that captures the relatedness among tasks, and utilize the optimal partitioning results of this graph to enhance the multi-task learning. The learning results in turn adjust the hidden graph structure. This process is iteratively repeated until convergence. Figure 4.1 intuitively demonstrates such process. We first randomly initialize a graph and hence its affinity matrix $\mathbf{A}$. We then solve the optimal partition $\mathbf{M}$ over $\mathbf{A}$. Following that, our designed $\mathbf{W}$ can be inferred based on both of $\mathbf{A}$ and $\mathbf{M}$. We ultimately leverage $\mathbf{W}$ to tune $\mathbf{A}$. The above process is repeated until $\mathbf{W}$ converges.

4.3.3 GROUPING STRUCTURE LEARNING

Given a graph $\mathbf{G}$ and its corresponding affinity matrix $\mathbf{A}$, we need to obtain its optimal partition $\mathbf{M}$. The quality of graph partition is usually measured by the so-called modularity metric [121]. Modularity was designed to calculate the strength of division of a graph into groups. Graph partitions with high modularity have dense connections between nodes within groups but sparse connections between nodes in different groups. We use the modularity to optimize the graph

---

[2]Support set of vertices is defined as a set of nodes that falls into the specific subgraph.

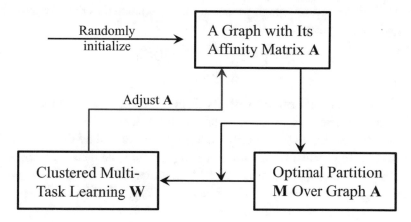

Figure 4.1: Automatical learning process of our model.

partitioning problem.

$$Q(\mathbf{M}) = \sum_{c^i \in \mathcal{G}}^{\mathcal{G}} \left[\frac{H(G_{c^i}, G_{c^i})}{H(G, G)} - \left(\frac{H(G_{c^i}, G)}{H(G, G)} \right)^2 \right], \tag{4.1}$$

where $H(G_{c^i}, G_{c^i})$ denotes the sum of the edges that fall within the given groups and is mathematically defined as $\sum_{i \in \sigma(c^i), i \in \sigma(c^i)} A_{ii}$; $H(G_{c^i}, G)$ measures the sum of weights over all edges attached to nodes in group $\mathbf{c}^i$ and is formulated as $\sum_{i \in \sigma(c^i), j \in \mathbb{N}^T} A_{ij}$; and $H(G, G) = \sum_{i \in \mathbb{N}^T, j \in \mathbb{N}^T} A_{ij}$ is a normalization term that measures the weights sum of all edges, where $\mathbb{N}^T = \{1, 2, \ldots, T\}$. Based on the above definition, we can further restate Eq. (4.1) as,

$$
\begin{aligned}
Q(\mathbf{M}) &\propto \sum_{c^i \in \mathcal{G}}^{\mathcal{G}} \left[H(G_{c^i}, G_{c^i}) H(G, G) - (H(G_{c^i}, G))^2 \right] \\
&= \sum_{c^i \in \mathcal{G}}^{\mathcal{G}} \left[\left(\frac{|\sigma(\mathbf{c}^i)|^2}{2} \mathbf{c}^{i^T} \mathbf{A} \mathbf{c}^i \right) \cdot \left(\frac{1}{2} \mathbf{e}^T \mathbf{A} \mathbf{e} \right) - \left(\frac{|\sigma(\mathbf{c}^i)|}{2} \mathbf{c}^{i^T} \mathbf{A} \mathbf{e} \right)^2 \right] \\
&= tr(\mathbf{A} \mathbf{E}) \cdot tr\left(\mathbf{S}^T \mathbf{A} \mathbf{S} \right) - tr\left(\mathbf{S}^T \mathbf{A} \mathbf{E} \mathbf{A} \mathbf{S} \right) \\
&= tr\left(\mathbf{S}^T (\mathbf{H} - \mathbf{B}) \mathbf{S} \right),
\end{aligned} \tag{4.2}
$$

where $\mathbf{S} = \mathbf{M}(\mathbf{M}^T \mathbf{M})^{-1} \in \mathbb{R}^{T \times K}$ is an index matrix such that $S_{ij} = 1$ if the i-th task belongs to the j-th group; and 0 otherwise. $\mathbf{e}$ and $\mathbf{E}$ are the vector and matrix of all ones, respectively. $tr(.)$ is trace norm. We can see that $\mathbf{M}$ is a column-wise normalized matrix of $\mathbf{S}$. Once we obtain $\mathbf{S}$, we can naturally derive $\mathbf{M}$; Thereinto, K is the number of clusters. Meanwhile, we denote $\mathbf{H} = tr(\mathbf{A} \mathbf{E}) \mathbf{A}$ and $\mathbf{B} = \mathbf{A} \mathbf{E} \mathbf{A}$ to simplify the expression of $Q(\mathbf{M})$ in Eq. (4.2).

The task to find the optimal graph partition can be expressed as the problem of maximizing the Q function with constraints:

$$\max_{\mathbf{S}} \quad tr\left(\mathbf{S}^T(\mathbf{H}-\mathbf{B})\mathbf{S}\right)$$
$$s.t. \quad \mathbf{S}^T\mathbf{S} = \mathbf{C} \preceq T, \tag{4.3}$$

where $\mathbf{C} \in \mathbb{R}^{K \times K}$ is a diagonal matrix with its diagonal component as $|\sigma(\mathbf{c}_i)|$. $\preceq$ denotes the element-wise inequality, and T is the number of vertices or tasks.

The optimization of Eq. (4.3) is an NP-hard problem, caused by the binary value property of the index matrix $\mathbf{S}$. To obtain a good approximating solution, we relax the entries of $\mathbf{S}$ to probabilistic values. In particular, we denote $\boldsymbol{\Lambda} \in \mathbb{R}^{K \times K}$ as a diagonal matrix. The diagonal elements of $\boldsymbol{\Lambda}$ are the Lagrangian multiplier of $\mathbf{S}^T\mathbf{S}$, i.e., $\lambda_{c_1}, \ldots, \lambda_{c_K}$. We then equally rewrite Eq. (4.3) by considering the Lagrangian configuration as,

$$\max_{\mathbf{S},\boldsymbol{\Lambda}} L(\mathbf{S}, \boldsymbol{\Lambda}) = tr\left(\mathbf{S}^T(\mathbf{H}-\mathbf{B})\mathbf{S}\right) - tr\left((\mathbf{S}^T\mathbf{S}-\mathbf{C})\boldsymbol{\Lambda}\right). \tag{4.4}$$

Taking derivative of Eq. (4.4) with respect to $\mathbf{S}$ and setting it to zero, we can reach the following eigenvalue systems,

$$(\mathbf{H}-\mathbf{B})\mathbf{S} = \mathbf{S}\boldsymbol{\Lambda}. \tag{4.5}$$

We can see that $\mathbf{S}$ and $\boldsymbol{\Lambda}$ are the set of eigenvectors and eigenvalues of matrix $(\mathbf{H}-\mathbf{B})$, respectively. We can thus obtain the analytic solution of $\mathbf{S}$ and hence $\mathbf{M}$.

4.3.4   EFFICIENT CLUSTERED MULTI-TASK LEARNING

Instead of uniform relatedness, we design a graph-regularized term to characterize the pairwise task relatedness. The reason for this is that the predicting functions of two strongly related tasks should be similar. It is formally stated as,

$$\Omega_{global}(\mathbf{W}) = \sum_{i,j=1}^{t} A_{ij}||\mathbf{w}_i - \mathbf{w}_j||^2 = tr\left(\mathbf{W}\mathbf{L}\mathbf{W}^T\right), \tag{4.6}$$

where $\mathbf{L}$ is a Laplacian matrix and is defined as $\mathbf{L} = \mathbf{D} - \mathbf{A}$; $\mathbf{D}$ is the degree matrix and is stated as $\mathbf{D} = diag(d_1, \ldots, d_T)$, where $d_i = \sum_{j=1}^{T} A_{ij}$; $||.||$ is Frobenius norm. As compared to the existing clustered multi-task learning methods [145], this term takes the weak relations across different clusters into consideration.

To strengthen the relatedness within the same group and quantify the compactness of these groups, we propose a metric to measure the task variances within clusters:

$$\Omega_{intra}(\mathbf{W}) = \sum_{c^i \in \mathcal{G}} \sum_{j \in \sigma(c^i)}^{|\sigma(c^i)|} ||\mathbf{w}_j^i - \bar{\mathbf{w}}^i||^2$$
$$= tr\left(\mathbf{W}\left(\mathbf{I}_T - \mathbf{M}\left(\mathbf{M}^T\mathbf{M}\right)^{-1}\mathbf{M}^T\right)\mathbf{W}^T\right), \tag{4.7}$$

where $\mathbf{w}_j^i$ represents the coefficient of the j-th task in the i-th group $\mathbf{c}_i$; $\bar{\mathbf{w}}^i = \frac{\sum \mathbf{w}_j^i}{|\sigma(\mathbf{c}^i)|}$ refers to the mean coefficients of all the tasks involved in $\mathbf{c}^i$; and $\mathbf{I}_T \in \mathbb{R}^{T \times T}$ is an identity matrix.

In contrast to the intra-cluster regularization, we propose a measure of between-cluster variance, which quantifies how close to each other the different clusters are:

$$\Omega_{inter}(\mathbf{W}) = \sum_{c^i, c^j \in \mathcal{G}, i < j}^{\mathcal{G}} ||\bar{\mathbf{w}}^i - \bar{\mathbf{w}}^j||^2$$
$$= tr\left(\mathbf{W}\mathbf{M}(K\mathbf{I}_K - \mathbf{E})\mathbf{M}^T\mathbf{W}^T\right), \tag{4.8}$$

where $\mathbf{I}_K \in \mathbb{R}^{K \times K}$ is an identity matrix, and $\mathbf{E} \in \mathbb{R}^{K \times K}$ is a matrix with all its entries being ones. Considering the squared loss function,[3] we can reach the following expression,

$$\mathcal{L}(\mathbf{W}) = \sum_{t=1}^{T} ||\mathbf{y}^t - \mathbf{X}\mathbf{w}_t||^2 = ||\mathbf{Y} - \mathbf{X}\mathbf{W}||^2, \tag{4.9}$$

where $\mathbf{W} = [\mathbf{w}_1, \ldots, \mathbf{w}_T] \in \mathbb{R}^{D \times T}$ denotes the coefficient matrix for the T tasks that we aim to learn.

Jointly integrating the above terms, we can reach the final objective function,

$$\min_{W} \mathcal{L}(\mathbf{W}) + \lambda_1 \Omega_{global}(\mathbf{W}) + \lambda_2 \Omega_{intra}(\mathbf{W}) - \lambda_3 \Omega_{inter}(\mathbf{W}) + \lambda_4 ||\mathbf{W}||^2. \tag{4.10}$$

Thereinto, we have four key parameters in our objective function. The first parameter λ_1 weights the graph-regularized term which considers the pairwise task relatedness. The second one enforces a clustering of tasks toward their mean when λ_2 increases, which quantifies the compactness of the clusters. The third parameter λ_3 controls the between-cluster variance, which is helpful to widen the distance between two clusters to avoid the negative transfer among dissimilar tasks. And the last parameter λ_4 is used to penalize the generalized errors to avoid the overfitting.

Taking the derivative of Eq. (4.10) with respect to $\mathbf{W}$, we have,

$$\frac{\partial Obj}{\partial \mathbf{W}} = 2\mathbf{X}^T\mathbf{X}\mathbf{W} - 2\mathbf{X}^T\mathbf{Y} + 2\lambda_1 \mathbf{W}\mathbf{L}^T + 2\lambda_4 \mathbf{W}$$
$$+ 2\lambda_2 \mathbf{W}\left(\mathbf{I}_T - \mathbf{S}\mathbf{M}^T\right) - 2\lambda_3 \mathbf{W}\left(\mathbf{M}(K\mathbf{I}_K - \mathbf{E})\mathbf{M}^T\right)$$
$$= -2\mathbf{X}^T\mathbf{Y} + 2\mathbf{U}\mathbf{W} + 2\mathbf{W}\mathbf{V}, \tag{4.11}$$

We can derive the closed-form solution of $\mathbf{W}$ as,

$$vec(\mathbf{W}) = \left(\mathbf{I}_T \otimes \mathbf{U} + \mathbf{V}^T \otimes \mathbf{I}_D\right) \cdot vec\left(\mathbf{X}^T\mathbf{Y}\right), \tag{4.12}$$

---

[3]The squared loss usually yields good performance as the other complex loss functions. We thus adopt loss as the loss function in our algorithm for simplicity and efficiency.

where the $\mathbf{I}_T \in \mathbb{R}^{T \times T}$ and $\mathbf{I}_D \in \mathbb{R}^{D \times D}$ are identify matrices; $\otimes$ means the operator of Kronecker product; $vec(\cdot)$ denotes the vector-version of matrix stacking the column into a vector. Meanwhile, we define $\mathbf{U} \in \mathbb{R}^{D \times D}$ and $\mathbf{V} \in \mathbb{R}^{T \times T}$ as follows,

$$\mathbf{U} = \mathbf{X}^T\mathbf{X} + \lambda_4\mathbf{I}_D,$$
$$\mathbf{V} = \lambda_1\mathbf{L}^T + \lambda_2\left(\mathbf{I}_T - \mathbf{M}\left(\mathbf{M}^T\mathbf{M}\right)^{-1}\mathbf{M}^T\right) - \lambda_3\mathbf{M}\left(K\mathbf{I}_K - \mathbf{E}\right)\mathbf{M}^T. \qquad (4.13)$$

Once we have obtained $\mathbf{W}$, we utilize it to adjust the grouping structure. The process is detailed in Algorithm 3.

Algorithm 3 Jointly learning the hidden grouping structure and the tasks

---
Input: $\lambda_1, \lambda_2, \lambda_3, \lambda_4, \mathbf{X}, \mathbf{Y}$
Output: $\mathbf{W}$
1: Initialize $t = 0$; and randomize $\mathbf{A}(t)$
2: **while** $\mathbf{W}(t)$ does not converge **do**
3:      get the optimal $\mathbf{M}(t)$ based on $\mathbf{A}(t)$
4:      get $\mathbf{W}(t + 1)$ via Eq. (4.12) given $\mathbf{A}(t)$,$\mathbf{M}(t)$
5:      construct $\mathbf{A}_{ij}(t + 1)$ via $\exp(\frac{\|\mathbf{w}_i(t+1)-\mathbf{w}_j(t+1)\|^2}{\theta^2})$
6:      set $t = t + 1$
7: **end while**

4.4   EXPERIMENTATION

4.4.1   EXPERIMENTAL SETTINGS

In this work, we applied the proposed *FLUTE* model to an emerging application scenario: user interest mining from social media. In particular, users explicitly indicate their multiple interests in their LinkedIn profiles. According to our statistics, on average each user has 4.25 interests based on thousands of user samples. On the other hand, users' historical posts on some social sites can be employed to characterize their interests and preferences. We regard this application as a multi-task learning problem, where each interest is aligned with a task. We assume there exists a hidden graph over these interests, which is able to capture their pairwise relatedness.

Although we are studying a mono-source multi-task learning problem, we still build a general data collection that can also be utilized to verify the multi-source multi-task learning models. To construct the benchmark dataset, we need to first tackle the problem of "social account alignment," which aims to identify the same users across different social networks by linking their multiple social accounts [1]. To accurately establish this mapping, we employed the emerging social service—Quora, which encourages users to explicitly list their multiple social accounts in their Quora profiles.[4] We collected candidates from Quora by the breadth-first-search method.

---
[4]One representative example can be seen via https://www.quora.com/Martijn-Sjoorda.

In the end, we harvested 172,235 Quora user profiles and only retained those who provided their Facebook, Twitter, and LinkedIn accounts in their Quora profiles. Based on these mappings, we launched a crawler to collect their historical social content, including their basic profiles, social posts, and relations.

To build the ground truth, we employed the structural information of users' Linkedin profiles: "Additional Information," which usually contains information about users' personal interests. User interests listed in their LinkedIn profiles are usually represented by phrases separated by comma, which facilitates the ground truth construction to a large extent. To obtain the representative interests, we filtered out the interests that are liked by fewer than 15 users. Finally, we obtained 74 interests.[5] Then we only retained those users who expressed these interests in their LinkedIn profiles and obtained 1,607 users ultimately. Table 4.1 lists the top 20 interests that are frequently preferred by users.

Table 4.1: Part of interests and their corresponding frequencies in the benchmark dataset

ID	Interest	Frequency	ID	Interest	Frequency
1	music	11	333	seo	94
2	entrepreneurship	199	12	hiking	90
3	marketing	176	13	running	85
4	blogging	162	14	web development	79
5	new technology	161	15	skiing	79
6	startups	139	16	networking	78
7	design	115	17	web design	77
8	cooking	112	18	politics	77
9	programming	112	19	snowboarding	74
10	internet	100	20	business	70

4.4.2   FEATURE EXTRACTION

To informatively describe users, we extracted two kinds of features: user topics and contextual topics.

- **User topics.** We explored the topic distributions of users' social posts to infer user interests. We generated topic distributions using Latent Dirichlet Allocation (LDA) [15], which has been widely found to be useful in latent topic modeling [24, 52]. Based on perplexity [69],

---

[5]These interests are available at http://msmt.farbox.com/.

we ultimately obtained 89, 24, 119 dimensional topic-level features respectively over users' Twitter,[6] Facebook,[7] and Quora[8] data.

- **Contextual topics.** We define users' contextual topics as the topics of users' connections. Like the saying, "birds of a feather flock together," we believe that the contextual topics intuitively reflect the contexts of users and further disclose their interests. Particularly, we studied followee connections on Twitter because of their intuitive reflection of topics that users are concerned with. As the bio descriptions are usually provided by users to briefly express themselves and may indicate users' summarized interests, we merged the bio descriptions of a user's followees into a document, on which we further applied the LDA model. We utilized the perplexity to tune the dimensions of topic-level features over these bio documents and obtained a 64 dimensional feature space. In this work, we only explored the contextual topics on Twitter, since the bio descriptions are usually missing on Facebook and Quora. In addition, LDA-based topic-level features were extracted from Facebook, Twitter, and Quora to represent each user, respectively. The corresponding feature dimensions are respectively 24, 89, and 119.

4.4.3   EVALUATION METRIC

It is well-known that for the inference problem, precision is usually much more important than recall [86]. We adopted two metrics that are able to capture the precision from different aspects. The first one is average $S@K$ over all testing users, which measures the probability of finding a relevant interest among the top K recommended items. To be more specific, for each testing user, $S@K$ is assigned 1 if a correct interest is ranked in the top K positions and 0 otherwise. The second is the average $P@K$ that stands for the proportion of recommended interests that are correct. $P@K$ is defined as

$$P@K = \frac{|\mathcal{C} \bigcap \mathcal{R}|}{|\mathcal{C}|}, \tag{4.14}$$

where $\mathcal{C}$ is a set of top K interests and $\mathcal{R}$ is the set of correct ones. Besides precision, we also measure the model efficiency in terms of CPU-Time, representing the time spent in executing the model.

All experiments were conducted over a server equipped with Intel(R) Xeon(R) CPU X5650 at 2.67GHZ, 48GB RAM, 24 cores, and 64-bit CentOS 5,4 operating system.

4.4.4   PARAMETER TUNING

We randomly split the user samples into two parts, 80% for training and the rest for testing. As mentioned earlier, we have four key parameters in Eq. (4.10). The optimal values of these

---

[6]Users' Twitter data refers to users' historical tweets.

[7]Users' Facebook data refers to users' historical timelines.

[8]Users' Quora data refers to users' historical questions and answers.

parameters were carefully tuned in the training data. In particular, to learn the optimal parameters, we conducted a grid search between 10^{-2} to 10^2 with small but adaptive step size. In particular, the step size was 0.01, 0.05, 0.5, and 5 for the range of [0.01,0.1], [0.1,1], [1,10], and [10,100], respectively. The parameters corresponding to the best $P@K$ were used to report the final results. For other comparing systems, the procedures to tune the parameters are analogous to ensure fair comparison. We have released the parameter configurations used in the models here.[9]

Figure 4.2 demonstrates the sensitivities of our model to the four key parameters, when fixing three parameters and tuning the remaining one. From these four sub-figures, we have the following observations: 1) The optimal parameters for one source is not applicable to the others. Therefore, we have to tune the parameters for Quora, Twitter, and Facebook sources, separately. 2) The performance on Facebook is much more stable as compared to other two sources. This reveals that the grouping structure over Facebook has a demonstrable effect.

Noticeably, we tuned the K in $S@K$ and $P@K$ from 1 to 10 and reported the optimal performance. The $P@K$ reaches the maximum at $K = 1$ for all sources; while $K = 3$, 10, and 4 are much preferable for Twitter, Facebook, and Quora in terms of $S@K$, respectively.

4.4.5   MODEL COMPARISON

To verify the effectiveness and efficiency of our proposed model, we compared it against the following state-of-the-arts models:

- *MTL-lasso*: The multi-task lasso model with least squared loss is widely used to reduce model complexity and achieve feature learning [115].

- *MTL-$\ell_{2,1}$*: The second baseline is the multi-task learning with group sparsity [5, 6]. This model captures the task relatedness by constraining all models to share a common set of features.

- *CMTL*: It is a representative clustered multi-task learning model, which is able to learn a grouping structure using gradient-descent solution. As reported in [145], this method outperforms all the traditional clustered multi-task learning models. Hence, we only selected this strongest one among the clustered multi-task learning models for comparison.

Table 4.2 shows the performance comparison between the baselines and our proposed model. From this table, we observed the following: (1) The last two clustered multi-task learning models significantly and consistently outperform the first two multi-task learning models across three different social sources. This verifies that the task relatedness is non-uniform and structure-regularized task relatedness is necessary. (2) Our proposed model and *CMTL* almost achieve comparable precision in terms of $S@K$ and $P@K$ on different sources, but our model is remarkably faster than *CMTL*. (3) The CPU-Time for 24-D Facebook, 89-D Twitter, and 119-D Quora is 32, 160, and 545, respectively. This implies that the efficiency of our model is highly

---

[9]https://FLUTE.farbox.com

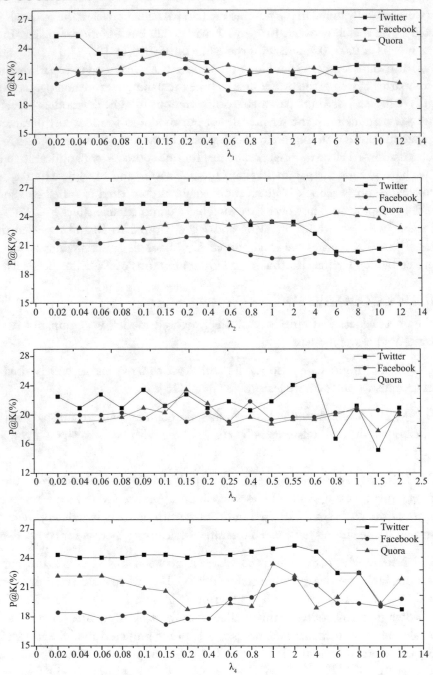

Figure 4.2: The performance of user interest mining by fixing three parameters and varying the remaining one.

correlated to the feature dimension. This finding motivates us to reduce the feature dimension before learning.

Table 4.2: Performance comparison among various models with non-pre-specific structure. $P@K$ and $S@K$ are measured in terms of percentage. "time" denotes "cpu-time."

	Twitter			Facebook			Quora		
	$P@K$	$S@K$	time	$P@K$	$S@K$	time	$P@K$	$S@K$	time
MTL-lasso	20.94	39.69	00.78	17.19	68.44	0.078	21.88	32.82	0.078
MTL-12, 1	15.63	34.06	0.078	17.19	66.88	0.032	19.69	28.44	0.078
CMTL	24.06	43.44	1113	21.56	67.82	997	23.44	33.13	961
FLUTE	25.31	43.44	160	21.88	68.75	32	24.38	32.82	545

4.4.6 NECESSITY OF STRUCTURE LEARNING

To justify the necessity of automatic structure learning, we compared the following settings:

- *Internal-MTL*: The graph structure over interests was pre-specified based on the external Web knowledge. In particular, we viewed each interest as a query and submitted it to the Google search engine. We collected the top 10 webpages, and then employed the library of BoilerPipe[10] to extract main contents from the returned webpages. Therefore, each interest can be represented by a document, based on which Bag-of-words model with TF-IDF term weighting scheme can be applied and the similarities among interests can be calculated. In such way, we can obtain $\mathbf{A}$.

- *External-MTL*: The graph structure over interests was pre-defined based on their normalized co-occurrence in users' LinkedIn profiles in our dataset. We can also get the affinity matrix $\mathbf{A}$.

- *FLUTE*: Our model automatically discovered the hidden grouping structure to enhance the learning performance.

The first two settings pre-constructed the fixed graph structures over interests. Their affinity matrix $\mathbf{A}$'s were fed into this model $\min_{\mathbf{W}} ||\mathbf{Y} - \mathbf{XW}||_F^2 + \rho_1 \sum_{i,j} A_{ij}||\mathbf{w}_i - \mathbf{w}_j||^2$.

Table 4.3 summarizes the comparison results. From this table, it can be seen that: (1) The first setting achieves the worst performance. This result implies that the graph structures based on internal knowledge have much stronger capabilities to capture the interest relatedness. (2) The setting under our model performs better than the first two settings. Several possible reasons lead to such a result. First, the structures of interests may depend on users' social content, rather than

---

[10]https://code.google.com/p/boilerpipe/.

Table 4.3: The precision comparison between the predefined/fixed structures and the automatic discovered structures

	Twitter		Facebook		Quora	
	P@K	*S@K*	*P@K*	*S@K*	*P@K*	*S@K*
Internal-MTL	25.31	35.94	20.31	68.13	21.56	32.19
External-MTL	23.16	34.69	20.63	68.44	21.25	31.88
FLUTE	25.31	35.31	21.88	68.75	24.38	32.82

the similarities or co-occurrences between the interest concepts. Second, the hidden grouping structure and the multi-task learning model can enhance each other in an automatic way. Third, the predefined and fixed structures may not capture the real relatedness among interests.

4.5   SUMMARY

This chapter presented a novel and efficient clustered multi-task learning model. It automatically discovers the hidden grouping structures of a given dataset, and utilizes such structure to capture and model the task relatedness. Tasks within the same groups are encouraged to share more knowledge, while those across groups are regarded as dissimilar tasks, among which knowledge transfer is penalized. The closed-form solution of desired tasks adjusts the grouping structures, and the refined structure reinforces the learning performance. We have verified our proposed model on a real-world application, i.e., user interest inference. The experimental results on publicly accessible dataset have well validated the promising efficiency and effectiveness of our model.

CHAPTER 5

Multi-source Multi-task Learning

5.1 APPLICATION: USER INTEREST INFERENCE FROM MULTI-SOURCE

In Chapter 4, we have studied user interest inference from a single source. In fact, we recently have witnessed many people with diverse interests involving in multiple social networks simultaneously. Multiple social networks comprehensively convey user interests from different view points. For instance, users may update their daily interests on Facebook, follow accounts of interest on Twitter, and ask or answer questions they are interested on Quora. Thus, fusing cues from multiple sources can potentially boost the performance of user interest inference by a large margin.

Inferencing user interests from multiple social networks, however, is non-trivial due to the following reasons. (a) **Source Integration**. Although users' behaviors on heterogeneous social networks describe their interests from different views, they should capture the essence or characteristics of the same user consistently. Therefore, how to effectively and comprehensively fuse them is one tough challenge. (b) **Interest Relatedness Characterization**. Interests are usually not independent but correlated in a nonuniform way. For example, given a set of interests $\mathcal{I} = \{basketball, football, travel, cooking\}$, the relatedness between *basketball* and *football* may be stronger than that between *basketball* and *cooking*. Given that in our dataset, most users who like to play basketball are more likely to spend their spare time on football than cooking. In the context of user interest inference, each interest is usually aligned with one task. Consequently, the second challenge is how to capture and characterize the relatedness among tasks and how to incorporate this into multi-task learning. (c) **Task-Sharing Features**. Not all the features are descriptive and discriminant for all the tasks. Identifying the useful task-sharing features effectively is of essential importance to user interest inference. This thus poses another crucial challenge for us.

It is noticeable that there are three lines of research dedicated to the problem of user interest inference. One is mono-source mono-task learning [91]. In this context, neither the relatedness among tasks nor the complementary information across sources is explored. Another line of effort is mono-source multi-task learning [125]. They take the task relatedness into account to boost the learning performance and alleviate the problem of insufficient training samples that the traditional single task learning faces. It has been observed that learning multiple related tasks simultaneously can improve the modeling accuracy and lead to a better learning performance, especially in cases where only a limited number of positive training samples exist for each task [35].

The third category of approaches is multi-source mono-task learning [1, 2]. Instead of sticking to a single source, they propose to aggregate multiple sources to infer user interests. It should be noted that the last two categories of approaches have weaknesses: existing mono-source multi-task learning explores the relatedness among tasks, but overlooks the consistency among different sources of a single task; whereas existing multi-source mono-task learning ignores the value of the label information of the other related tasks.

As an improvement to the existing works, we propose a **Structure-constrained Multi-sOurce multi-tasK lEarning** (*SMOKE*) scheme to infer user interests. In particular, our scheme jointly regularizes two important aspects. One is the source consistency. The rationale is that interests reflected by different social networks for the same person should be similar, and hence the disagreement among the prediction results should be penalized. The other is the tree-guided task relatedness modeling. Based on prior knowledge, we organize all the tasks (interests) into a tree structure, which can effectively capture various relatedness among tasks. Specifically, the tree structure settles all tasks in leaf nodes and characterizes the relatedness among them by internal nodes. Moreover, the higher the level the internal node is located, the weaker is the relatedness imposed on its children tasks. This is accomplished by a tree-guided group lasso regularizer. Meanwhile, *SMOKE* learns representative features for groups of related tasks. A potential benefit of sharing training instances among tasks is that the data scarcity problem can be alleviated. Extensive experiments on a real-world dataset well validated our scheme. We have released our compiled dataset,[1] which will facilitate other researchers to repeat our approach and to comparatively verify their own ideas.

5.2   RELATED WORK

The problem of user interest inference from multiple social networks exhibits dual-heterogeneities: each task (interest) corresponds to features from multiple sources. Toward this end, the most related work lies in the area of multi-view multi-task learning. The authors of this work [46] proposed a graph-based iterative framework for multi-view multi-task learning (*IteM*2) in the context of text classification. Given task pairs, *IteM*2 projects them to a new Reproducing Kernel Hilbert Space based upon the common views they share. However, this is a transductive model, which fails to generate predictive models on independent and unknown samples. To deal with the intrinsic trouble of transductive models, the work in [136] presents an inductive multi-view multi-task learning model (*regMVMT*). It employs a co-regularization term to achieve model consistency on unlabeled samples from different views. Meanwhile, another regularization function is utilized across multiple tasks to guarantee that the learned models are similar. Noticeably, the implicit assumption that all tasks are uniformly related without prior knowledge might be inappropriate. Realizing this limitation, the authors proposed a revised model (*regMVMT+*) that incorporates a component to automatically infer the task relatedness. As a generalized model of *regMVMT*, an inductive convex shared structure learning algorithm for multi-view multi-task

---

[1]The compiled dataset is currently publicly accessible via: `http://msmt.farbox.com/`.

problem (*CSL-MTMV*) was developed in [58]. *CSL-MTMV* considers the shared predictive structure among multiple tasks.

Notably, only a limited number of works have been published regarding multi-view multi-task learning and few of them have been applied to user interest inference. Different from these existing methods which maximize the agreement between views using unlabeled data, *SMOKE* works toward supervised learning with two advantages: (1) *SMOKE* considers source consistency and tree-guided relatedness among tasks simultaneously; and (2) *SMOKE* allows the learning of task-sharing features using weighted group lasso, where the weights can be learned from prior knowledge.

5.3   MULTI-SOURCE MULTI-TASK LEARNING

5.3.1   NOTATION

Suppose we have a set of N labeled data samples, $S \geq 2$ sources and $T \geq 2$ tasks. Let D_s denote the number of features extracted from the s-th source. Let $\mathbf{X}_s \in \mathbb{R}^{N \times D_s}$ denote the feature matrix generated from source s, and each row represents a user sample. The feature dimension extracted from all these sources is thus $D = \sum_{s=1}^{S} D_s$. The whole feature matrix can be written as $\mathbf{X} = \{\mathbf{X}_1, \mathbf{X}_2, \cdots, \mathbf{X}_S\} \in \mathbb{R}^{N \times D}$. The label matrix can be represented as $\mathbf{Y} = \{\mathbf{y}_1, \mathbf{y}_2, \cdots, \mathbf{y}_T\} \in R^{N \times T}$, where $\mathbf{y}_t = (y_t^1, y_t^2, \cdots, y_t^N)^T \in R^N$ corresponds to the label vector regarding the t-th task.

5.3.2   PROBLEM FORMULATIONS

For each task, we can learn S predictive models, each of which is generated from one source and defined as follows,

$$\mathbf{f}_{st}(\mathbf{X}_s) = \mathbf{X}_s \mathbf{w}_{st}, \tag{5.1}$$

where $\mathbf{w}_{st} = (w_{st}^1, w_{st}^2, \cdots, w_{st}^{D_s})^T \in \mathbb{R}^{D_s}$ represents the linear mapping function for the t-th task with respect to the s-th source. Let $\mathbf{W} = (\mathbf{w}_1, \mathbf{w}_2, \cdots, \mathbf{w}_T) \in \mathbb{R}^{D \times T}$ denote the whole linear mapping block matrix, where $\mathbf{w}_t = (\mathbf{w}_{1t}, \mathbf{w}_{2t}, \cdots, \mathbf{w}_{St})^T \in \mathbb{R}^D$. The final predictive model for task t can be reinforced via linear combination of these S models. Without the prior knowledge of source confidence, we treat all sources equally as follows,

$$\mathbf{f}_t(\mathbf{X}) = \sum_{s=1}^{S} \frac{1}{S} \mathbf{f}_{st}(\mathbf{X}_s). \tag{5.2}$$

In multi-class problems, tasks are usually inter-correlated. Multi-source multi-task learning is thus proposed to model their relatedness while seamlessly integrating multiple sources. To select discriminant features, group lasso is considered in the component of multi-task learning. Let $\mathbf{W} = (\mathbf{w}_1, \mathbf{w}_2, \cdots, \mathbf{w}_T) \in \mathbb{R}^{D \times T}$ denote the linear mapping block matrix, where $\mathbf{w}_t =$

$(\mathbf{w}_{1t}^T, \mathbf{w}_{2t}^T, \cdots, \mathbf{w}_{St}^T)^T \in \mathbb{R}^D$. The multi-source multi-task learning with group lasso can be formalized as follows,

$$\Gamma = \frac{1}{2N} \sum_{t=1}^{T} \left\| \mathbf{y}_t - \sum_{s=1}^{S} \frac{1}{S} \mathbf{X}_s \mathbf{w}_{st} \right\|^2 + \frac{\lambda}{2} \sum_{s=1}^{S} \sum_{d=1}^{D_s} \left\| \mathbf{w}_s^d \right\|, \qquad (5.3)$$

where $\mathbf{w}_s^d = (w_{s1}^d, w_{s2}^d, \cdots, w_{sT}^d)$, $\sum_{s=1}^{S} \sum_{d=1}^{D_s} \left\| \mathbf{w}_s^d \right\| = \left\| \mathbf{W} \right\|_{2,1}$ and λ is the nonnegative regularization parameter that regulates the sparsity of the solution regarding $\mathbf{W}$. When $T \geq 2$, the weights of one feature across all tasks are first grouped by the L_2 norm, and all features are then grouped by the L_1 norm. Thus, the $L_{2,1}$ norm penalty is able to select features based on their strength over all tasks. In this way, we can simultaneously learn the task-sharing features. Obviously, when $T = 1$, this formulation reduces to a typical problem of Lasso [115].

However, the above optimization problem simply assumes that all the tasks share a common set of relevant input features, which might be unrealistic in many real word scenarios. For example, in our work, the tasks "basketball" and "football" tend to share a common set of relevant input features, which are less likely to be useful for the task "cooking." This consideration motivates us to assume that the relatedness among different tasks can be characterized by a tree $\mathcal{T}$ with a set of nodes $\mathcal{V}$. In particular, the leaf nodes represent all the tasks, while the internal nodes denote the groupings of leaf nodes. Intuitively, each node $v \in \mathcal{V}$ of the tree $\mathcal{T}$ can be associated with group G_v, which consists of all the leaf nodes (tasks) belonging to the subtree rooted at node v. Moreover, the higher level the internal node is located at, the weaker relatedness it controls. The root of $\mathcal{T}$ is assigned the highest level. To characterize such strength of relatedness among tasks, we assign a weight e_v to each node $v \in \mathcal{V}$ according to the prior knowledge via a hierarchical agglomerative clustering algorithm [105]. As illustrated in Figure 5.1, it is apparent that the tasks "basketball" and "football" are more correlated as compared to the task "cooking." Thus, in Figure 5.1, the tasks "basketball" and "football" are first grouped in node v_4 with a weight $e_{v_4} = 0.6$. Then these two tasks are grouped in a higher level internal node v_5, whose weight $e_{v_5} = 0.4$, together with the task "cooking."

We mathematically formulate the source integration and tree-constrained[2] group lasso into one unified model,

$$\Gamma = \frac{1}{2N} \sum_{t=1}^{T} \left\| \mathbf{y}_t - \sum_{s=1}^{S} \frac{1}{S} \mathbf{X}_s \mathbf{w}_{st} \right\|^2 + \frac{\lambda}{2} \sum_{s=1}^{S} \sum_{d=1}^{D_s} \sum_{v \in \mathcal{V}} e_v \left\| \mathbf{w}_{sG_v}^d \right\|, \qquad (5.4)$$

where $\mathbf{w}_{sG_v}^d$ is a vector of coefficients $\{w_{st}^d : t \in G_v\}$. In addition, we assume that the mapping functions from all sources agree with one another as much as possible. Therefore, we introduce the regularization term to model the result consistency among different sources. The final objective

---

[2]Beyond tree-structure, our model is extendable to incorporate other structures, such as graph.

function $\boldsymbol{\Gamma}$ is restated as follows,

$$\frac{1}{2N}\sum_{t=1}^{T}\left\|\mathbf{y}_t - \sum_{s=1}^{S}\frac{1}{S}\mathbf{X}_s\mathbf{w}_{st}\right\|^2 + \frac{\lambda}{2}\sum_{s=1}^{S}\sum_{d=1}^{D_s}\sum_{v\in\mathcal{V}}e_v\left\|\mathbf{w}_{sG_v}^d\right\|$$

$$+ \frac{\mu}{2N}\sum_{t=1}^{T}\sum_{s=1}^{S}\sum_{s'\neq s}\left\|\mathbf{X}_s\mathbf{w}_{st} - \mathbf{X}_{s'}\mathbf{w}_{s't}\right\|^2, \tag{5.5}$$

where μ is the nonnegative regularization parameter that regulates the disagreement among models learned from different sources.

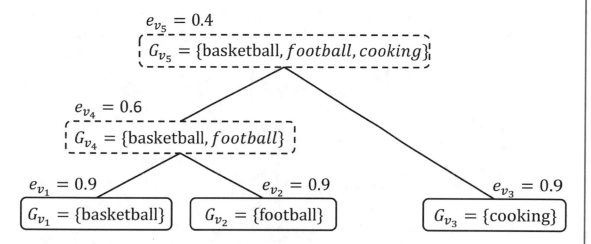

Figure 5.1: Illustration of inter-interests relatedness in a tree structure.

5.3.3   OPTIMIZATION

Considering that the second term in Eq. (5.5) is not differentiable, we use an equivalent formulation of it, which has been proven by [61], to facilitate the optimization as follows,

$$\frac{\lambda}{2}\left(\sum_{s=1}^{S}\sum_{d=1}^{D_s}\sum_{v\in\mathcal{V}}e_v\left\|\mathbf{w}_{sG_v}^d\right\|\right)^2. \tag{5.6}$$

Still, the $L_{2,1}$ norm in the above formulation gives rise to a non-convex function, which makes it intractable to solve directly. Therefore, we further resort to another variational formulation [6] of Eq. (5.6). According to the Cauchy-Schwarz inequality, given an arbitrary vector $\mathbf{b} \in \mathbb{R}^M$ such that $\mathbf{b} \neq \mathbf{0}$, we have,

$$
\begin{aligned}
\sum_{i=1}^{M} |b_i| &= \sum_{i=1}^{M} \theta_i^{\frac{1}{2}} \theta_i^{-\frac{1}{2}} |b_i| \\
&\leq \left(\sum_{i=1}^{M} \theta_i \right)^{\frac{1}{2}} \left(\sum_{i=1}^{M} \theta_i^{-1} b_i^2 \right)^{\frac{1}{2}} \\
&\leq \left(\sum_{i=1}^{M} \theta_i^{-1} b_i^2 \right)^{\frac{1}{2}},
\end{aligned}
\tag{5.7}
$$

where θ_i's are introduced variables that should satisfy $\sum_{i=1}^{M} \theta_i = 1, \theta_i > 0$ and the equality holds for $\theta_i = |b_i| / \|\mathbf{b}\|_1$. Based on this preliminary, we can derive the following inequality,

$$
\begin{aligned}
\left(\sum_{s=1}^{S} \sum_{d=1}^{D_s} \sum_{v \in \mathcal{V}} e_v \|\mathbf{w}_{sG_v}^d\| \right)^2 &\\
&\leq \sum_{s=1}^{S} \frac{\left(\sum_{d=1}^{D_s} \sum_{v \in \mathcal{V}} e_v \|\mathbf{w}_{sG_v}^d\| \right)^2}{q_s} \\
&\leq \sum_{s=1}^{S} \sum_{d=1}^{D_s} \frac{\left(\sum_{v \in \mathcal{V}} e_v \|\mathbf{w}_{sG_v}^d\| \right)^2}{q_{s,d}} \\
&\leq \sum_{s=1}^{S} \sum_{d=1}^{D_s} \sum_{v \in \mathcal{V}} \frac{e_v^2 \|\mathbf{w}_{sG_v}^d\|^2}{q_{s,d,v}},
\end{aligned}
\tag{5.8}
$$

where we introduce the variable $q_{s,d,v}$. The equality can be attained if $q_{s,d,v}$ satisfies that,

$$
q_{s,d,v} = \frac{e_v \|\mathbf{w}_{sG_v}^d\|}{\sum_{s=1}^{S} \sum_{d=1}^{D_s} \sum_{v \in \mathcal{V}} e_v \|\mathbf{w}_{sG_v}^d\|}.
\tag{5.9}
$$

Consequently, minimizing $\boldsymbol{\Gamma}$ is equivalent to minimizing the following convex objective function,

$$
\begin{aligned}
&\frac{1}{2N} \sum_{t=1}^{T} \left\| \mathbf{y}_t - \sum_{s=1}^{S} \frac{1}{S} \mathbf{X}_s \mathbf{w}_{st} \right\|^2 + \frac{\lambda}{2} \sum_{s=1}^{S} \sum_{d=1}^{D_s} \sum_{v \in \mathcal{V}} \frac{e_v^2 \|\mathbf{w}_{sG_v}^d\|^2}{q_{s,d,v}} \\
&+ \frac{\mu}{2N} \sum_{t=1}^{T} \sum_{s=1}^{S} \sum_{s' \neq s} \left\| \mathbf{X}_s \mathbf{w}_{st} - \mathbf{X}_{s'} \mathbf{w}_{s't} \right\|^2.
\end{aligned}
\tag{5.10}
$$

To facilitate the computation of the derivative of objective function $\boldsymbol{\Gamma}$ with respect to $\mathbf{w}_{st}$, we define a diagonal matrix $\mathbf{Q}_{st} \in \mathbb{R}^{D_s \times D_s}$ as follows,

$$Q_{st}(d, d) = \sum_{v:t \in G_v} \frac{e_v^2}{q_{s,d,v}}. \tag{5.11}$$

Finally, we have the following objective function,

$$\frac{1}{2N} \sum_{t=1}^{T} \left\| \mathbf{y}_t - \sum_{s=1}^{S} \frac{1}{S} \mathbf{X}_s \mathbf{w}_{st} \right\|^2 + \frac{\lambda}{2} \sum_{t=1}^{T} \sum_{s=1}^{S} \mathbf{w}_{st}^T \mathbf{Q}_{st} \mathbf{w}_{st}$$

$$+ \frac{\mu}{2N} \sum_{t=1}^{T} \sum_{s=1}^{S} \sum_{s' \neq s} \left\| \mathbf{X}_s \mathbf{w}_{st} - \mathbf{X}_{s'} \mathbf{w}_{s't} \right\|^2. \tag{5.12}$$

We adopt the alternating optimization strategy to solve Eq. (5.12) [60]. Particularly, we alternatively optimize $\mathbf{w}_{st}$ and $q_{s,d,v}$, where we optimize one variable with the other one fixed in each iteration and keep this iterative procedure until the objective value converges.

When $q_{s,d,v}$ is fixed, we take the derivative of objective function $\boldsymbol{\Gamma}$ regarding $\mathbf{w}_{st}$ as follows,

$$\frac{\partial \boldsymbol{\Gamma}}{\partial \mathbf{w}_{st}} = \frac{1}{NS} \mathbf{X}_s^T \left(\sum_{s=1}^{S} \frac{1}{S} \mathbf{X}_s \mathbf{w}_{st} - \mathbf{y}_t \right) + \lambda \mathbf{Q}_{st} \mathbf{w}_{st} + \sum_{s \neq s'} \frac{\mu}{N} \mathbf{X}_s^T \left(\mathbf{X}_s \mathbf{w}_{st} - \mathbf{X}_{s'} \mathbf{w}_{s't} \right). \tag{5.13}$$

Setting Eq. (5.13) to zero and rearranging the terms, we derive that all $\mathbf{w}_{st}$'s can be learned jointly by the following linear system given a task t,

$$\mathbf{L}_t \mathbf{w}_t = \mathbf{b}_t,$$

$$\begin{bmatrix} \mathbf{L}_{11} & \mathbf{L}_{12} & \mathbf{L}_{13} & \cdots & \mathbf{L}_{1S} \\ \mathbf{L}_{21} & \mathbf{L}_{22} & \mathbf{L}_{23} & \cdots & \mathbf{L}_{2S} \\ \mathbf{L}_{31} & \mathbf{L}_{32} & \mathbf{L}_{33} & \cdots & \mathbf{L}_{3S} \\ \vdots & \vdots & \vdots & \ddots & \vdots \\ \mathbf{L}_{S1} & \mathbf{L}_{S2} & \mathbf{L}_{S3} & \cdots & \mathbf{L}_{SS} \end{bmatrix} \begin{bmatrix} \mathbf{w}_{1t} \\ \mathbf{w}_{2t} \\ \mathbf{w}_{3t} \\ \vdots \\ \mathbf{w}_{St} \end{bmatrix} = \begin{bmatrix} \mathbf{b}_{1t} \\ \mathbf{b}_{2t} \\ \mathbf{b}_{3t} \\ \vdots \\ \mathbf{b}_{St} \end{bmatrix}, \tag{5.14}$$

where $\mathbf{L}_t \in \mathbb{R}^{D \times D}$ is a sparse block matrix with $S \times S$ blocks, $\mathbf{w}_t \in \mathbb{R}^D$ and $\mathbf{b}_t \in \mathbb{R}^D$ are both sparse block matrices with S blocks. $\mathbf{L}_{ss}$, $\mathbf{L}_{ss'}$, and $\mathbf{b}_{st}$ are defined as,

$$\begin{cases} \mathbf{L}_{ss} &= \frac{1}{NS^2} \mathbf{X}_s^T \mathbf{X}_s + \frac{\mu(S-1)}{N} \mathbf{X}_s^T \mathbf{X}_s + \lambda \mathbf{Q}_{st}, \\ \mathbf{L}_{ss'} &= \frac{1}{NS^2} \mathbf{X}_s^T \mathbf{X}_{s'} - \frac{\mu}{N} \mathbf{X}_s^T \mathbf{X}_{s'}, \\ \mathbf{b}_{st} &= \frac{1}{NS} \mathbf{X}_s^T \mathbf{y}_t. \end{cases} \tag{5.15}$$

According to the definition of positive-definite matrix, $\mathbf{L}_t$ can be easily proven to be positive definite and invertible. Then we can derive the closed-form solution of $\mathbf{w}_t$ as follows,

$$\mathbf{w}_t = \mathbf{L}_t^{-1} \mathbf{b}_t. \tag{5.16}$$

Furthermore, we notice that $\mathbf{w}_t$ can be computed individually, which saves considerable space and time cost. Meanwhile, we optimize $q_{s,d,v}$ according to Eq. (5.9) with fixed $\mathbf{w}_t$. The overall procedures for alternating optimization are summarized in Algorithm 4.

Algorithm 4 Alternating optimization for solving Eq. (5.12)

Input: $\mathbf{X}, \mathbf{y}, \lambda, \mu$
Output: $\mathbf{W}$
 1: Initialize $(\mathbf{W})^0$ by fitting each source individually on the available data.
 2: **for** $k = 1, 2, \cdots$ **do**
 3:    **for** $t = 1, 2, \cdots, T$ **do**
 4:       **for** $s = 1, 2, \cdots, S$ **do**
 5:          Update $(\mathbf{Q}_{st})^k$ according to Eq. (5.9) and (5.11).
 6:       **end for**
 7:    **end for**
 8:    **for** $t = 1, 2, \cdots, T$ **do**
 9:       Compute each $(\mathbf{w}_t)^k$ according to Eq. (5.16).
 10:   **end for**
 11:   **if** the objective value stops decreasing **then**
 12:      return $\mathbf{W} = (\mathbf{W})^k$
 13:   **end if**
 14: **end for**

5.3.4   CONSTRUCTION OF INTEREST TREE STRUCTURE

We aim to employ the hierarchical agglomerative clustering algorithm to construct the tree structure. One challenge is that an interest is usually represented by a single concept, which makes it hard to measure the similarities among interests and apply the hierarchical agglomerative clustering algorithm. Toward this end, two types of prior knowledge are utilized.

(1) **External source**. We exploit an external source—the Web, where a huge amount of prior knowledge about interests are encoded implicitly. We transform each interest into a query and submit it to Google search engine. We collect the top 10 webpages, and then employ the library of BoilerPipe[3] [61] to extract clean main contents from the returned webpages. Therefore, each interest can be represented by a document, based on which Bag-of-words model [82] with TF-IDF term weighting scheme [103] can be applied and the similarities among interests can be evaluated.

(2) **Internal source**. Although the external source provides us the general prior knowledge, we believe that the internal prior knowledge stored in our dataset also plays a vital role in user interest inference. Driven by this consideration, we propose to measure the similarities among interests

---

[3]https://code.google.com/p/boilerpipe/

based on their co-occurrence in users' LinkedIn profiles in our dataset.[4] It deserves attention that we exploit all available LinkedIn profiles that exhibit users' personal interests rather than that of the subset of users selected for the task of interest inference. Suppose we have a set of interests $\mathcal{I} = \{In_1, In_2, \cdots, In_T\}$, and a set of documents $\mathcal{DD} = \{d_1, d_2, \cdots, d_N\}$, where d_l contains all interests of user l. Let $c(j, k, l) = 1$ if and only if interests In_j and In_k both occur in d_l, and $c(j, k, l) = 0$ otherwise. Then the co-occurrence matrix $\mathbf{H}$ is defined as follows,

$$H(j, k) = \begin{cases} \frac{\sum_l c(j,k,l)}{\sum_j \sum_l c(j,k,l)} & \text{if } j \neq k; \\ 1 & \text{otherwise.} \end{cases} \tag{5.17}$$

Each row of $\mathbf{H}$ corresponds to the co-occurrence of an interest with others. Then we use the JensenShannon divergence [16] to measure the similarities among interests.

It is suggested to apply the hierarchical agglomerative clustering algorithm on these enriched interests and build the tree structure. To assign appropriate weights to nodes, we choose to utilize the normalized height h_v of a subtree rooted at node v to characterize its weight e_v, where $e_v = 1 - h_v$. Such an assignment guarantees the aforementioned condition that the higher node corresponds to the weaker relatedness. It is noted that we normalize the heights for all nodes such that the root node is at height 1. We thus derive two models *SMOKE-e* and *SMOKE-i* based on two types of prior knowledge, respectively.

5.4 EXPERIMENTS

5.4.1 EXPERIMENTAL SETTINGS

In this work, we casted the problem of user interest inference as the structure constrained multi-source multi-task learning problem. In particular, we explored four popular social networks: Twitter, Facebook, Quora, and LinkedIn, where the features were extracted from the first three sources and the ground truth was constructed based on the last one.

We verified our model on a publicly accessible dataset as described in Chapter 4. Figure 5.2 shows the user frequency distribution with respect to the number of interests over this dataset. Similarly, we employed the same precision metrics, $S@K$ and $P@K$, to measure the performance of our model and the competitors. $S@K$ represents the mean probability that a correct interest is captured within the top K recommended interests; while $P@K$ stands for the proportion of the top K recommended interests that are correct.

All the experiments were conducted over a server equipped with Intel(R) Xeon(R) CPU X5650 at 2.67 GHZ on 48 GB RAM, 24 cores, and 64-bit CentOS 5.4 operating system.

5.4.2 MODEL COMPARISON

To justify the effectiveness of our proposed model *SMOKE*, we compared it with the following five state-of-the-art baselines:

---

[4]Users may list a set of personal interests in their LinkedIn profiles.

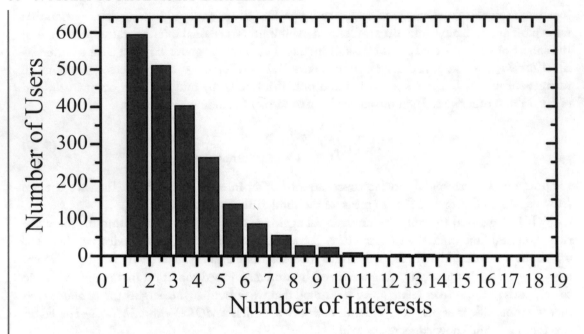

Figure 5.2: User frequency distribution with respect to the number of interests over our dataset.

- *SVM*: The first baseline is a traditional single-source, single-task learning method—support vector machine (SVM) [27], which simply concatenates the features generated from different sources into a single feature vector and learns each task individually. We chose the learning formulation with the kernel of radial-basis function, implemented based on LIB-SVM [21].

- *RLS*: The second baseline is the regularized least squares (RLS) model [59], which also learns each task individually and aims to minimize the objective function of $\frac{1}{2N} \left\| \mathbf{y}_t - \sum_{s=1}^{S} \frac{1}{S} \mathbf{X}_s \mathbf{w}_{st} \right\|^2 + \frac{\lambda}{2} \left\| \mathbf{w}_t \right\|^2$.

- *regMVMT*: The third baseline is the regularized multi-view multi-task learning model, introduced in [136]. This model regulates both the source consistency and the task relatedness. However, it simply assumes the uniform relatedness among tasks.

- *SMOKE-eu*: The fourth baseline is a derivation of *SMOKE-e*. This method constructs the tree structure based on external source in the same manner as *SMOKE-e* but assigns uniform weights to all nodes.

- *SMOKE-iu*: The fifth baseline is a derivation of *SMOKE-i*, which constructs the tree structure using internal source but weights all nodes uniformly.

We adopted the grid search strategy to determine the optimal values for the regularization parameters. Experimental results reported in this work are the average values over 10-fold cross validation. Noticeably, we tuned the K in $S@K$ and $P@K$ from 1 to 10 and reported the optimal performance for each fold. Generally, the $S@K$ reaches the maximum at $K = 10$, while $K = 1$ is much preferable regarding $P@K$.

Table 5.1 shows the performance comparison between baselines and our proposed scheme. We observed that *SMOKE*-i and *SMOKE*-e both outperform the single source single task learning *SVM* and *RLS*. This verifies the significance of considering source consistency and task relatedness simultaneously. Moreover, it is not unexpected that *SVM* achieves the worst performance. A possible explanation might be the insufficient positive training samples for certain interests. For example, only 24 positive training samples are available for the interest "surfing." In addition, the less satisfactory performance of *regMVMT*, as compared to *SMOKE*-i and *SMOKE*-e, confirms that it is advisable to characterize the task relatedness in a tree structure instead of correlating all tasks uniformly. Besides, *SMOKE-i* and *SMOKE-e* show superiority over *SMOKE-iu* and *SMOKE-eu* respectively, which enables us to draw a conclusion that modeling the relatedness strength among tasks merits our particular attention. Last but not least, *SMOKE*-i performs better than *SMOKE*-e. This finding demonstrates the importance of prior knowledge extracted from our internal source.

Table 5.1: Performance comparison among various models. They were fed with features extracted from multiple sources.

Approaches	P@K (%)	S@K (%)
SVM	8.69	54.69
RLS	24.32	73.86
regMVMT	24.69	74.54
SMOKE-eu	25.50	73.80
SMOKE-iu	24.56	74.11
SMOKE-e	**25.72**	**74.57**
SMOKE-i	**26.50**	**74.85**

Based on the practical results, the time complexity of *regMVMT* is remarkably higher than that of *SMOKE*. In particular, *regMVMT* costs about 562 seconds to execute, 114 times of that taken by *SMOKE* for each iteration. This is mainly attributed to the computation of the inverse of a matrix with dimension of DT, which requires a time complexity of $O(D^3T^3)$. Compared to *SMOKE*, it is rather time consuming using *regMVMT*.

Table 5.2: Contribution of individual social network and their various combinations

Social Network Combinations	P@K (%)	S@K (%)
Twitter	24.75	73.05
Facebook	19.59	69.74
Quora	20.97	68.19
Twitter + Facebook	25.51	74.98
Twitter + Quora	24.89	74.41
Facebook + Quora	22.52	71.80
Twitter + Facebook + Quora	**26.50**	**74.85**

5.4.3   SOURCE COMPARISON

To shed light on the descriptiveness of multiple social network integration, we conducted experiments over various source combinations.

Table 5.2 shows the performance of *SMOKE-i* over individual social network and their various combinations. We noted that the more sources we incorporated, the better the performance can be achieved. This suggests the complementary relationships instead of mutual conflicting relationships among the sources. Moreover, we found that aggregating data from all these three social networks can achieve better performance as compared to each of the single source. Interestingly, we observed that *SMOKE* over Twitter alone achieves a much better performance, as compared to that using Quora or Facebook alone. This may be caused by that we additionally extracted contextual topics apart from user topics in Twitter, which can reveal user interests more directly. It is far from incomprehensible that *SMOKE* would degenerate to multi-task learning when the context problem involves only one single source.

5.4.4   COMPLEXITY DISCUSSION

To analyze the complexity of *SMOKE*, we need to estimate the time cost in terms of constructing $\mathbf{Q}$, $\mathbf{L}_t$, and $\mathbf{b}_t$, defined in Eq. (5.11) and Eq. (5.15), as well as computing the inverse of $\mathbf{L}_t$. Assuming $D \gg S$, the construction of diagonal matrix $\mathbf{Q}$ has a time complexity of $O(DT)$, and the construction of matrix $\mathbf{L}_t$ has a time complexity of $O(ND^2)$. Due to the fact that the time cost of matrix multiplication $\mathbf{X}_s^T \mathbf{X}_{s'}$ and that of constructing $\mathbf{b}_t$ involved in Eq. (5.15) remain the same for all iterations and $\mathbf{L}_t$ is symmetric, we can reduce the practical time consumption remarkably. In addition, computing the inverse of $\mathbf{L}_t$ has the complexity of $O(D^3)$ by the standard method. Then the total complexity should be $O(D^3T)$. We notice that the speed bottleneck lies in the number of features and the number of tasks instead of the number of data samples. As D is usually small, *SMOKE* should be computationally efficient.

5.5   SUMMARY

This chapter presents a structure-constrained multi-source multi-task learning scheme in the context of user interest inference. In particular, this scheme takes both the source consistency and the tree-guided task relatedness into consideration by introducing two regularizations to the objective function. Moreover, the proposed model is able to effectively select the task-sharing features by employing the weighted group lasso. Notably, the weights can be learned from two kinds of prior knowledge: external source and internal source. Experimental results demonstrate the effectiveness of our proposed scheme.

CHAPTER 6

Multi-source Multi-task Learning with Feature Selection

6.1 APPLICATION: USER ATTRIBUTE LEARNING FROM MULTIMEDIA DATA

In Chapter 5, we have extended multi-source mono-task learning and mono-source multi-task learning models to a unified multi-source multi-task learning model. It is capable of task-sharing feature selection via the weighted group lasso. However, it still fails to discriminate the task-specific features. In this chapter, we present an improved multi-source multi-task learning model, which is able to jointly learn the task-sharing and task-specific features. Most importantly, we will verify this model on a multimodal and multimedia dataset. Before we dive into it, let's consider the following application scenario: user attribute learning, in particular on the user occupation prediction.

Social media and mobile phones promote mutually. In particular, the development of social networking technologies has changed the role of mobile phones which apart from pure communication devices are also powerful devices for generating and consuming multimedia data [55]. The growing ubiquity of mobile phones has in turn led to a bright new stage of social multimedia services. In light of this, users are convenient to capture images and videos on the mobile end, associate them with social and contextual metadata such as tips and GPS tags, and disseminate them in the social platforms. Hence, social media and mobile users constitute an ideal platform for analyzing users' habits and behaviors, which also provide us the most influential sources in shaping user attributes, such as age, gender, occupation, and social status.

User attributes are crucial prerequisites for many interesting applications. We list a few examples. (1) Studying social roles and statuses is very helpful to gain the insights of the whole society as well as manage social resources at the individual level; (2) Age and gender inference substantially contributes in analyzing the users' profiles and conducting demographic statistics; (3) Interest and occupation prediction benefit the customized marketing and personalized recommendation, as well as social circle detection and activity recognition. Noticeably, a significant body of internet users might be reluctant to expose their attributes to the public. As an alternative, predicting user attributes from mobile social media is of great interest to both industry and academia.

Despite its value and significance, learning user attributes from mobile social media remains in its infancy due to the following challenges: (1) people may be involved in multiple mobile social media platforms for various purposes simultaneously. For example, people share their footprints with their friends using Foursquare network; meanwhile, they may also share the latest news using Twitter, and photos using Instagram. Different aspects of users are disclosed on different social networks due to their different emphases. However, these heterogeneous multimedia sources are complementary to each other and essentially characterize the same user from different perspectives. Effectively unifying and uncovering the information embedded in the heterogeneous social media sources remains a largely unaddressed research problem. (2) User attributes are typically correlated in a non-uniform way. Take a user's occupation prediction as an example. Given a set of occupations, $C = \{nurse; dentist; scientist; professor, cook\}$, the relatedness between nurse and dentist may be stronger than that between nurse and cook, since nurse and dentist work in similar environments, and they hence may discuss similar topics in their social forums and post images with similar context. (3) Features describing users may be in high dimension, but in fact not all features are discriminant. In fact, a subset of highly related attributes may share a common set of features, whereas weakly related attributes are less likely to be affected by the same features. In addition, individual attributes may have their unique discriminant features. In summary, learning attribute-sharing features and attribute-specific features effectively is significant to user attributes learning.

To address the aforementioned challenges, we propose a unified model, the so-called multi-Source mulTi-task leArning wiTh fUsed laSso (*STATUS*), to infer user attributes. As a research entry point, we specifically explore occupation prediction in this work. We assume that each user is involved in multiple social media platforms.[1] Our model treats each occupation as a task. It simultaneously co-regulates source consistency and task relatedness. In particular, for each given user, we first crawl his/her historical multimedia posts from multiple mobile platforms, including tweets from Twitter, check-in records from Foursquare, images from Instagram, as well as occupations from Linkedin (ground truth). The occupations revealed by different social networks for the same users should be similar, and also the inconsistency among the prediction results from individual sources should be penalized. On the other hand, the relatedness among occupations is encoded with the graph-guided fused lasso, where each task is represented by a node in a graph and the similarities between the tasks are captured via an adjacency matrix. The graph structure is constructed based on external and internal knowledge. As compared to the previous methods regrading all task pairs as equally related and cannot encode the hidden complicated relationships among tasks, our method uses graph-guided fused lasso penalty to encourage models for task pairs to be similar whenever they are connected in the graph network. In addition, the proposed *STATUS* model is capable of identifying discriminant task-specific and task-sharing features. As an added benefit, it is advantageous to learn tasks by leveraging cues from the other related tasks, especially when the data is scare. It can thus alleviate the problem of insufficient training samples.

---

[1]Even though some users do not have multiple social platforms, we can utilize matrix factorization techniques to complete the missing sources.

Also, our model can be generalizable to other attributes, such as interests, age groups, and social roles.

The contributions of this work can be summarized as: (1) we proposed a multi-source learning model with graph-guided fused lasso penalty to infer user occupations, which jointly regularizes source consistency and task relatedness; and (2) we relaxed the non-smooth objective function to a smooth one, theoretically demonstrated its solution, and practically analyzed its computational complexity.

6.2   RELATED WORK

Mobile social media platforms provide venues for diverse people to record and share their behaviors. Their online behaviors are representative of many aspects of their attributes. Hence predicting user attributes from social media is feasible and draws more and more attention [14, 89, 90, 95, 102, 113, 141]. Recent works focus on the inference of age [102], gender [30], race [83], occupation [96], personality [41], political alignment [26], and depression [29]. For example, the authors in [17] constructed a large, multilingual dataset labeled with gender and studied several statistical models for determining the gender of uncharacterized Twitter users. The work in [91] attempts to automatically infer the political orientation and ethnicity of given users by leveraging observable information such as the user behaviors, network structures, and the linguistic content of the users' Twitter feeds. The work introduced in [100] discovers four latent user attributes, including gender, age, regional origin, and political orientation, by a stacked-SVM-based classification algorithm over a rich set of original features extracted solely from informal content of Twitter. Furthermore, the authors in [133] extended the existing work on attribute inference by leveraging the principle of homophily. They evaluated the inference accuracy gained by augmenting the user features with features derived from the Twitter profiles and posts of friends. They considered three attributes which have varying degrees of assortativity: gender, age, and political affiliation. Choudhury et al. [29] studied the potential signals for the prediction of users' depression from social media, ranging from the decrease in social activities, raised negative effects, to greater expressions of religious involvement. Recently, the authors in [46] noticed that existing approaches for user attributes learning on social media are generally in supervised settings and they formulated a weakly supervised paradigm to extract user profiles from Twitter.

Even though considerable success has been achieved in earlier works, most of them learn user attributes from a single source and few explore the relatedness among the attributes. In fact, we are living in the era of multiple social networks, and users are hence involved in more and more social networks simultaneously. It is thus desirable to integrate multiple social media platforms to comprehensively characterize the same users. On the other hand, the relatedness among attributes can be learned from external knowledge, or can be manually defined based on prior knowledge. As an improved work, our model incorporates these two factors. In addition, we employ fused lasso to learn task-specific and task-sharing features.

6.3   DATA CONSTRUCTION

6.3.1   DATA CRAWLING STRATEGY

We utilized the following strategy to construct our multi-source data for the application of occupation inference:

1. We searched About.me with some manually selected occupation concepts. These occupations were selected from this alphabetical list.[2]

2. We removed those users who fail to list the following three social accounts in their About.me profile: Twitter, Linkedin, and Foursquare. For each of the rest of the users, we have his/her three URLs corresponding to the three social accounts. According to these criteria, we collected a set of 3,180 users.

3. For each of these 3,180 users, we collected all their historical posts from Linkedin, Twitter, and Foursquare, respectively.

4. We also collected images from Instagram for these 3,180 users using the following procedure: if users provide their Instagram URL on About.me, we can directly crawl their images;[3] otherwise, based on the Foursquare check-ins, we collected photos related to the visited venues from Instagram. The venue is matched according to the identity between Foursquare and Instagram.[4] Users sometimes share their Instagram photos in their Twitter account with the snippet "instagram.com"; we thus collected them to enrich our image collection.

Table 6.1 shows the first-order statistics of our collected data from multiple sources. It is observable that each user on average posted more than 2,300 tweets. This indicates that the users with multiple social media accounts at the same time are usually very active. These four sources characterize users from different views. In particular, Linkedin, a professional networking platform, serves as the source of ground truth, where users typically post their professional and career information; Twitter is an online social networking service that enables users to send and read short 140-character messages called "tweets." Some of these tweets may signal occupation-related information. For instance, property agents may talk about rentals, stamp duty, and commission rates; Foursquare records users' travel histories, which can implicitly leak out the behaviors or patterns of ones' profession. Take professors and bankers as examples. Check-ins of professors primarily distribute in universities and conference venues; while the check-ins for bankers usually occur in financial institutions and central business districts. Images on Instagram can visually and intuitively characterize the users' work places.

---

[2]http://www.occupationsguide.cz/en/abecedni/abecedni.htm
[3]We observed **40.9%** of these 3,180 users also explicitly post their Instagram access in their About.me profile.
[4]http://instagram.com/developer/endpoints/locations/

Table 6.1: Statistics of our collected data from multiple sources, including tweets from Twitter, check-ins and tips from Foursquare, profiles from Linkedin, and photos from Instagram

Data Sources	Users	Tweets from Twitter	Check-ins from Foursquare	Tips from Foursquare	Profiles from LinkedIn	Images from Instagram
Statistics	3,180	7,365,373	28,504	22,079	3,180	106,684

6.3.2 GROUND TRUTH CONSTRUCTION

We leveraged the structural information of users' Linkedin profiles to establish the ground truth, which greatly saves the labor-intensive labeling process. Linkedin users usually formally list all their occupation experiences in the "Experience" block, as illustrated in Figure 6.1. According to our statistics, on average, each user in our dataset has 5.65 occupations. For each user, we extracted his/her occupation list to serve as the ground truth. In this way, we obtained 12,409 unique occupation titles. To avoid typos and unusual occupation titles, such as "meeting booster," we filtered out the occupation titles which occur fewer than five times, and we have 385 left. It is noteworthy that the vocabulary gap is very large for the occupation representation. Users with diverse backgrounds utilize various phrases to represent their titles. For instance, "programmer" and "software developer" are employed by different users to refer to the same "software engineer" title. We manually merged some variants. Ultimately, we have 80 occupation titles. Table 6.2 displays 20 representative occupations. Correspondingly, Figure 6.2 illustrates the user frequency distribution over these 20 occupations.

Table 6.2: This table lists 20 representative occupations in our dataset. In fact, we studied 80 occupations. To save the space, we do not list them all.

ID	Occupations	ID	Occupations
1	Sales/Markets	11	Writer
2	Software Engineer	12	Waiter
3	Founder/Cofounder	13	Artist
4	Consultant	14	Blogger
5	Web Designer	15	CTO
6	Researcher	16	Photographer
7	CEO	17	Product Manager
8	Project Manager	18	Teacher
9	Student	19	Editor
10	Agent	20	Investor

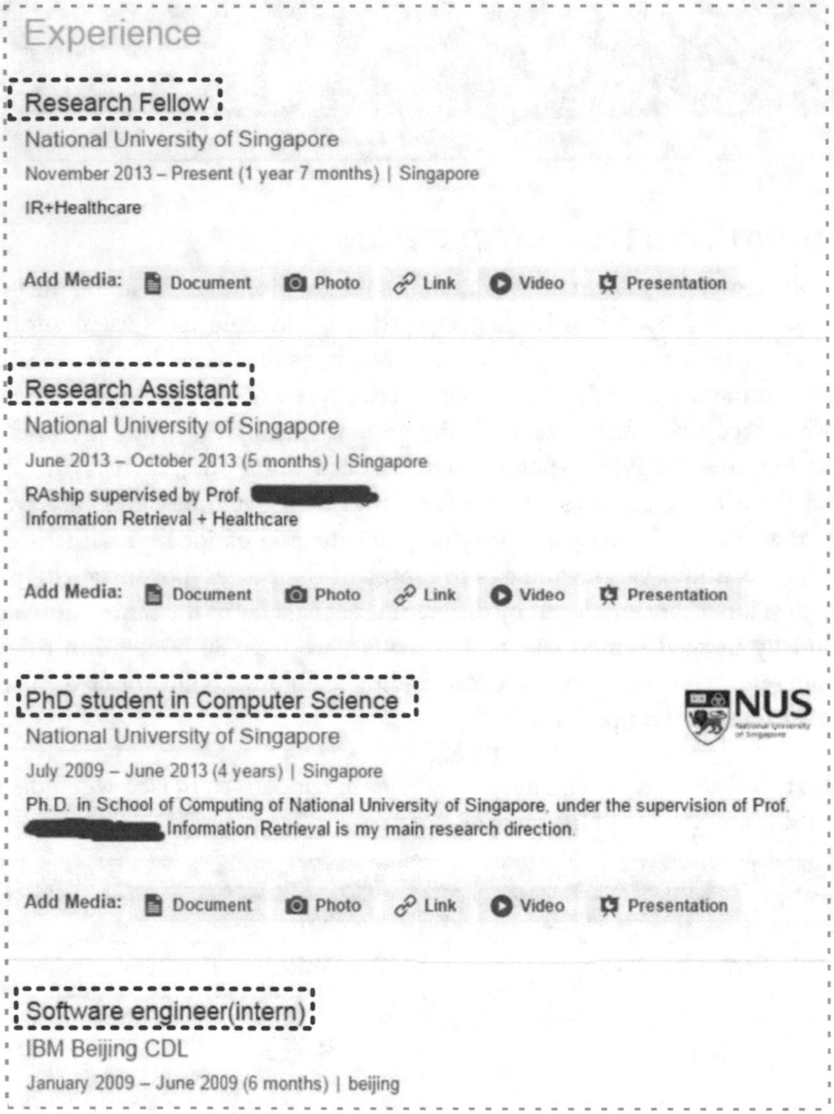

Figure 6.1: Demonstration of work experiences listed in Linkedin, i.e., occupation titles. They are highlighted by purple dotted rectangles. Due to privacy concerns, we concealed some personal information.

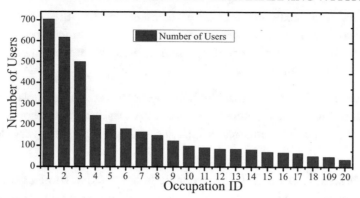

Figure 6.2: Illustration of occupation-user distributions in our dataset. The occupation ID is aligned with the occupation title in Table 6.2. We have 80 occupations, but we do not display them all due to space.

6.4   MULTI-SOURCE MULTI-TASK LEARNING WITH FUSED LASSO

Assume that we are given N users $\mathbf{X} = [\mathbf{x}_1, \mathbf{x}_2, ..., \mathbf{x}_N]^T$ in the training set, and their corresponding occupation categories $\mathbf{Y} = [\mathbf{y}_1, \mathbf{y}_2, ..., \mathbf{y}_C] \in \mathbb{R}^{N \times C}$. Each user is characterized by V complementary sources from V mobile media platforms. For example, the n-th user can be represented by $\mathbf{x}_n = [\mathbf{x}_{n1}^T, \mathbf{x}_{n2}^T, ..., \mathbf{x}_{nV}^T]^T$, where $\mathbf{x}_{nv} \in \mathbb{R}^{D_v}$, and D_v denotes the dimensionality of feature space on the v-th source. All the training samples on the v-th source and on all the sources are respectively represented as $\mathbf{X}_v = [\mathbf{x}_{1v}, \mathbf{x}_{2v}, ..., \mathbf{x}_{Nv}]^T \in \mathbb{R}^{N \times D_v}$ and $\mathbf{X} = [\mathbf{X}_1, \mathbf{X}_2, ..., \mathbf{X}_v] \in \mathbb{R}^{N \times D}$, where $D = \sum_{v=1}^{V} D_v$. Our objective is to generalize the *STATUS* model from training users to predict the occupations of other unseen users, given their information from multiple social media platforms.

We define $f_v^c(\mathbf{x}_{nv})$ as the probability function of user n falling into the c-th occupation category, estimated based on the v-th source. In a vector-wise form, the inference function of all users for the c-th occupation by leveraging the v-th source can be stated as,

$$\mathbf{f}_v^c(\mathbf{X}_v) = \mathbf{X}_v \mathbf{w}_{cv}, \qquad (6.1)$$

where $\mathbf{w}_{cv} \in \mathbb{R}^{D_v}$ is the coefficient vector for source v and task c. The probability for all users associated with c-th occupation is modeled by averaging the prediction results from all sources,

$$\mathbf{f}^c(\mathbf{X}) = \frac{1}{V} \sum_{v=1}^{V} \mathbf{f}_v^c(\mathbf{X}_v) = \frac{1}{V} \sum_{v=1}^{V} \mathbf{X}_v \mathbf{w}_{cv}. \qquad (6.2)$$

Based on the above definition, the traditional squared loss function that measures the empirical error on the training users can be formulated as, $\sum_{c=1}^{C} \| \mathbf{y}_c - \frac{1}{V} \sum_{v=1}^{V} \mathbf{X}_v \mathbf{w}_{cv} \|^2$. As reported in [124], the squared loss usually yields good performance as the other complex loss functions. We thus adopt the squared loss as the loss function in our algorithm for simplicity and efficiency.

To boost the occupation inference performance, besides the loss function, we simultaneously consider these three assumptions:

- *Source Consistency*. We assume that the heterogeneous social media platforms of the same users characterizing their behaviors from multiple views, but should consistently reflect the same occupation type. Mathematically, $\mathbf{f}_v^c(\mathbf{X}_v)$ should be the same or very close with $\mathbf{f}_u^c(\mathbf{X}_u)$, for $u \neq v$.

- *Graph-regularized Relatedness*. It is reasonable to assume that some of the occupations are often more closely related and more likely to share common relevant input features than other occupations. We assume that occupations are related in a complex manner in the form of a graph. It is noteworthy that tree and some other basic structures are the special cases of graph structure. The graph structure can be built based on the external and internal prior knowledge.

- *Feature Selection*. Feature sparsity is another reasonable assumption since only a small fraction of features are associated with their corresponding occupations. Feature selection using the ℓ_1 penalty (also referred as 1-norm or Lasso penalty) has been shown to perform well when there are spurious features mixed with relevant features, which enforces many parameters being zeros and the parameter vector is thus sparse. Lasso and its advanced variants, such as fused lasso, should be considered to select discriminative features.

By jointly considering these assumptions, the objective function $\Phi(\mathbf{w}_{cv})$ of occupation inference can be formulated as,

$$
\min_{\mathbf{w}_{cv}} \frac{1}{2} \sum_{c=1}^{C} \| \mathbf{y}_c - \frac{1}{V} \sum_{v=1}^{V} \mathbf{X}_v \mathbf{w}_{cv} \|^2 + \frac{\lambda}{2} \sum_{c=1}^{C} \sum_{v=1}^{V} \sum_{v' \neq v}^{V} \| \mathbf{X}_v \mathbf{w}_{cv} - \mathbf{X}_{v'} \mathbf{w}_{cv'} \|^2
$$

$$
+ \beta \sum_{e=(c,c')\in\mathcal{E}} r_{cc'} \sum_{v=1}^{V} \| \mathbf{w}_{cv} - \mathbf{w}_{c'v} \|_1 + \mu \sum_{c=1}^{C} \sum_{v=1}^{V} \| \mathbf{w}_{cv} \|_1 . \tag{6.3}
$$

The first term is the widely adopted least square loss function; the second term controls the source consistency; the third one implements the graph-guided fused lasso for multi-task classification that exploits the graph structure over the output variables; while the last term controls the sparsity. λ and β are parameters that respectively regularize the disagreement of heterogeneous sources for the same task and differences between related tasks on the same source. μ is a parameter that regulates the strength of the ℓ_1-norm regularization on multi-source multi-task learning function.

Graph construction is the key to our proposed graph-guided fused lasso penalty. In the desired graph, each node represents one task or occupation, and each edge connects two nodes with its weight indicating the strength of correlation between two nodes. Two tasks connected by an edge with a high weight tend to be influenced by the same set of features. To construct the graph, we leveraged two kinds of prior knowledge encoded in external and internal resources. For the external resource, we exploited the web information indexed by Google. In particular, we treated each occupation title as a query and submitted it to Google Search Engine. We collected the top 20 webpages for each occupation, and then utilized the BoilerPipe tool[5] to extract the clean content from the pages. The similarities between pairwise occupations were estimated by computing the corresponding pairwise document similarities. In addition to the external resource, we also explored the internal knowledge embedded in our collected dataset. To be more specific, we measured the co-occurrence in users' Linkedin profiles in our dataset. For the given occupation c and c', let's denote $\mathcal{U}_c$ and $\mathcal{U}_{c'}$ the sets of Linkedin profiles that respectively contain occupation c and c'. Inspired by the Jaccard coefficient [68], the relationship between these two occupations can be estimated by $\frac{|\mathcal{U}_c \cap \mathcal{U}_{c'}|}{|\mathcal{U}_c \cup \mathcal{U}_{c'}|}$. For pairwise occupations, their ultimate relationship was calculated by linearly averaging the similarity scores on the external and internal resources. We utilized $\mathbf{R}$ to denote the adjacency matrix of occupations, with its entry $r_{cc'}$ representing the relatedness between occupation c and c'. To avoid the commonly seen occupations overwhelming the non-commonly seen ones, we symetrically normalized $\mathbf{R}$ as $\mathbf{D}^{-\frac{1}{2}}\mathbf{R}\mathbf{D}^{-\frac{1}{2}}$, where $\mathbf{D}$ is a diagonal matrix whose (i,i)-th element is the sum of the i-th row of $\mathbf{R}$.

6.5   OPTIMIZATION

Our objective function $\Phi(\mathbf{w}_{cv})$ is convex, but the last two terms are non-smooth. Let's denote the last two terms as $\Psi_0(\mathbf{w}_{cv})$. We have,

$$
\Psi_0(\mathbf{w}_{cv}) = \beta \sum_{e=(c,c')\in\mathcal{E}} r_{cc'} \sum_{v=1}^{V} \parallel \mathbf{w}_{cv} - \mathbf{w}_{c'v} \parallel_1 + \mu \sum_{c=1}^{C} \sum_{v=1}^{V} \parallel \mathbf{w}_{cv} \parallel_1
$$

$$
= \beta \parallel \mathbf{WH} \parallel_1 + \mu \parallel \mathbf{W} \parallel_1 = \parallel \mathbf{WB} \parallel_1, \tag{6.4}
$$

where $\mathbf{B} = [\beta\mathbf{H}, \mu\mathbf{I}] \in \mathbb{R}^{C \times (C+|\mathcal{E}|)}$ and $\mathcal{E}$ is the graph edge set; $\mathbf{W}$ is a block matrix, $\mathbf{W} = [\mathbf{w}_1, \mathbf{w}_2, ..., \mathbf{w}_C] \in \mathbb{R}^{D \times C}$ and $\mathbf{w}_c = [\mathbf{w}_{c1}^T, \mathbf{w}_{c2}^T, ..., \mathbf{w}_{cV}^T]^T$. $\mathbf{H} \in \mathbb{R}^{C \times |\mathcal{E}|}$ is a variant vertex-edge incident matrix defined as below:

$$
H_{i,e} = \begin{cases} r_{cc'} & \text{if } e = (c,c') \text{ and } i = c; \\ -r_{cc'} & \text{if } e = (c,c') \text{ and } i = c'; \\ 0 & \text{otherwise.} \end{cases} \tag{6.5}
$$

---

[5] https://code.google.com/p/boilerpipe/

Since the dual norm of the entry-wise matrix ℓ_∞ norm is the ℓ_1 norm,[6] we can further restate the overall penalty in Eq. (6.4) as:

$$\Psi_0(\mathbf{w}_{cv}) = \| \mathbf{WB} \|_1$$

$$\equiv \max_{\|\mathbf{A}\|_\infty \leq 1} tr\left(\mathbf{A}^T \mathbf{WB}\right), \tag{6.6}$$

where $\| \cdot \|_\infty$ is the matrix entry-wise ℓ_∞ norm, defined as the maximum absolute value of all entries in the matrix; $\mathbf{A} \in \mathcal{P} = \{\mathbf{A} | \|\mathbf{A}\|_\infty \leq 1, \mathbf{A} \in \mathbb{R}^{D \times (C+|\mathcal{E}|)}\}$ is an auxiliary matrix associated with $\| \mathbf{WB} \|_1$; and $tr(\cdot)$ is the trace of a matrix.

The formulation in Eq. (6.6) is still a non-smooth function with respect to $\mathbf{w}_{cv}$, which leads to a tough challenge for the optimization. Toward this end, we construct an approximation of Eq. (6.6) with manageable errors. In particular, we define $\Psi_\gamma(\mathbf{w}_{cv})$ as,

$$\Psi_\gamma(\mathbf{w}_{cv}) = \Psi_0(\mathbf{w}_{cv}) + \frac{\gamma}{2} \| \mathbf{A} \|_F^2 . \tag{6.7}$$

Let ϵ denote the approximation error. We then have,

$$\begin{aligned}
\epsilon &= \Psi_\gamma(\mathbf{w}_{cv}) - \Psi_0(\mathbf{w}_{cv}) \\
&= \frac{\gamma}{2} \| \mathbf{A} \|_F^2 \\
&\leq \max_{\|\mathbf{A}\|_\infty \leq 1} \frac{\gamma}{2} \| \mathbf{A} \|_F^2 \\
&= \frac{\gamma}{2} D \times (C + |\mathcal{E}|).
\end{aligned} \tag{6.8}$$

We hence set the parameter γ as $\frac{2\epsilon}{D \times (C+|\mathcal{E}|)}$ to control the errors and to achieve the best convergence rate. In this work, we utilize $\Psi_\gamma(\mathbf{w}_{cv})$ to approximate $\Psi_0(\mathbf{w}_{cv})$.

By taking the derivative of $\Psi_\gamma(\mathbf{w}_{cv})$ over $\mathbf{A}$ and setting it to zero, we can derive $\mathbf{A} = \frac{\mathbf{WB}}{\gamma}$. We then apply $\mathbf{A}$ to $\mathcal{P}$, and we reach the optimal solution of $\mathbf{A}$,

$$\mathbf{A}^* = \Gamma\left(\frac{\mathbf{WB}}{\gamma}\right), \tag{6.9}$$

where Γ is a mapping function. It projects any $x \in \mathbb{R}$ into

$$\Gamma(x) = \begin{cases} 1 & \text{if } x > 1, \\ x & \text{if } -1 \leq x \leq 1, \\ -1 & \text{if } x < -1. \end{cases} \tag{6.10}$$

For a given matrix $\mathbf{A}$, $\Gamma(\mathbf{A})$ is defined as applying Γ on each of the entries in $\mathbf{A}$.

---

[6]https://wiki.sfu.ca/personal/aoberman/index.php/Norms_and_dual_norms

$\Psi_\gamma(\mathbf{w}_{cv})$ is a convex and continuously differentiable function with respect to $\mathbf{w}_{cv}$ for any $\gamma > 0$. We treat $\Psi_\gamma(\mathbf{w}_{cv})$ as a smooth approximation of $\Psi_0(\mathbf{w}_{cv})$. In particular, we have

$$
\frac{\partial \Psi_\gamma(\mathbf{w}_{cv})}{\partial \mathbf{w}_{cv}} = \frac{\partial tr\left(\mathbf{A}^{*T}\mathbf{W}\mathbf{B}\right)}{\partial \mathbf{w}_{cv}}
$$
$$
= \frac{\partial tr\left(\mathbf{W}\mathbf{B}\mathbf{A}^{*T}\right)}{\partial \mathbf{w}_{cv}}. \tag{6.11}
$$

Let's denote $\mathbf{Q} = \mathbf{B}\mathbf{A}^{*T}$, where $\mathbf{Q} = [\mathbf{q}_1, \mathbf{q}_2, ..., \mathbf{q}_C]^T \in \mathbb{R}^{C \times D}$ and $\mathbf{q}_c = [\mathbf{q}_{c1}^T, \mathbf{q}_{c2}^T, ..., \mathbf{q}_{cV}^T]^T$. We then can restate the above formulations as,

$$
\frac{\partial tr\left(\mathbf{W}\mathbf{Q}^T\right)}{\partial \mathbf{w}_{cv}} = \frac{\partial tr\left(\sum_{c=1}^{C} \mathbf{w}_c \mathbf{q}_c^T\right)}{\partial \mathbf{w}_{cv}}
$$
$$
= \frac{\partial tr\left(\mathbf{w}_c \mathbf{q}_c^T\right)}{\partial \mathbf{w}_{cv}}
$$
$$
= \frac{\partial tr\left(\mathbf{q}_c^T \mathbf{w}_c\right)}{\partial \mathbf{w}_{cv}}
$$
$$
= \frac{\partial tr\left(\sum_{v=1}^{V} \mathbf{q}_{cv}^T \mathbf{w}_{cv}\right)}{\partial \mathbf{w}_{cv}}
$$
$$
= \mathbf{q}_{cv}^T. \tag{6.12}
$$

Taking derivative of our objective function $\Phi(\mathbf{w}_{cv})$ in Eq. (6.3) over $\mathbf{w}_{cv}$, we obtain,

$$
\frac{\partial \Phi(\mathbf{w}_{cv})}{\partial \mathbf{w}_{cv}} = \frac{1}{V}\mathbf{X}_v^T\left(\frac{1}{V}\sum_{v=1}^{V}\mathbf{X}_v\mathbf{w}_{cv} - \mathbf{y}_c\right) + \lambda\mathbf{X}_v^T\sum_{v'\neq v}^{V}\left(\mathbf{X}_v\mathbf{w}_{cv} - \mathbf{X}_{v'}\mathbf{w}_{cv'}\right) + \mathbf{q}_{cv}^T. \tag{6.13}
$$

By rearranging the term orders of Eq. (6.13), we arrive at,

$$
\frac{1}{V}\mathbf{X}_v^T\mathbf{y}_c - \mathbf{q}_{cv}^T = \left\{\frac{1}{V^2}\mathbf{X}_v^T\mathbf{X}_v + \lambda(V-1)\mathbf{X}_v^T\mathbf{X}_v\right\}\mathbf{w}_{cv} + \left(\frac{1}{V^2} - \lambda\right)\mathbf{X}_v^T\sum_{v'\neq v}^{V}\mathbf{X}_{v'}\mathbf{w}_{cv'}. \tag{6.14}
$$

To facilitate the optimization analysis, we define some notations and rewrite Eq. (6.14) in the following form,

$$
\mathbf{L}\mathbf{w}_c = \mathbf{t}^c. \tag{6.15}
$$

The above formulation is equivalent to the following linear system,

$$
\begin{bmatrix}
\mathbf{L}_{11} & \mathbf{L}_{12} & \mathbf{L}_{13} & \cdots & \mathbf{L}_{1V} \\
\mathbf{L}_{21} & \mathbf{L}_{22} & \mathbf{L}_{23} & \cdots & \mathbf{L}_{2V} \\
\mathbf{L}_{31} & \mathbf{L}_{32} & \mathbf{L}_{33} & \cdots & \mathbf{L}_{3V} \\
\vdots & \vdots & \vdots & \ddots & \vdots \\
\mathbf{L}_{V1} & \mathbf{L}_{V2} & \mathbf{L}_{V3} & \cdots & \mathbf{L}_{VV}
\end{bmatrix}
\begin{bmatrix}
\mathbf{w}_{c1} \\
\mathbf{w}_{c2} \\
\mathbf{w}_{c3} \\
\vdots \\
\mathbf{w}_{cV}
\end{bmatrix}
=
\begin{bmatrix}
\mathbf{t}_1^c \\
\mathbf{t}_2^c \\
\mathbf{t}_3^c \\
\vdots \\
\mathbf{t}_V^c
\end{bmatrix},
\tag{6.16}
$$

where each involved element is defined as,

$$
\begin{cases}
\mathbf{t}_v^c = \frac{1}{V}\mathbf{X}_v^T \mathbf{y}_c - \mathbf{q}_{cv}^T, \\
\mathbf{L}_{vv} = \frac{1}{V^2}\mathbf{X}_v^T \mathbf{X}_v + \lambda(V-1)\mathbf{X}_v^T \mathbf{X}_v, \\
\mathbf{L}_{vv'} = \left(\frac{1}{V^2} - \lambda\right)\mathbf{X}_v^T \mathbf{X}_{v'}.
\end{cases}
\tag{6.17}
$$

$\mathbf{L}$ is a positive definite matrix and hence it is invertible [112, 113]. We can hence derive the closed-form solution of $\mathbf{w}_c$

$$
\mathbf{w}_c = \mathbf{L}^{-1}\mathbf{t}^c.
\tag{6.18}
$$

We iteratively calculate $\mathbf{W}$ and $\mathbf{A}$ until convergence. The initial values of $\mathbf{W}$ is generated by randomization. In the whole process of our iteration, each step decreases the objective function value $\Phi(\mathbf{w}_{cv})$, whose lower bound is zero and therefore the convergence of our model is guaranteed [77].

6.6 EXPERIMENTS

In this section, we conducted extensive evaluations to thoroughly verify our proposed model and each of its components.

6.6.1 EXPERIMENTAL SETTINGS

Data Preprocessing

We observed that the textual part of our dataset is of varying qualities. Some users may write meaningless tips at their check-in venues, and some suspicious users may leave spam on Twitter. Before feature extraction, we performed the following pre-processing steps on the textual parts to filter the noise and reduce the feature space:

- We converted all uppercase letters to lowercase ones, and all slang words to synonyms based on the external dictionary to reduce the number of possible terms;

- We eliminated texts with phone numbers or email addresses since they are generally spam;

- We removed all the non-alphanumeric characters to filter out the meaningless numbers;

- We removed stop words and those terms with frequencies less than five.

Evaluation Metrics

For the task of user occupation inference, precision is of more importance as compared to recall. We thus validated our model via two widely accepted metrics that are able to capture precision from different aspects. The first one is average $S@K$ over all testing users. The second one is average $P@K$. The definitions of $S@K$ and $P@K$ are detailed in Chapter 4.

Data Partition for Training and Testing

Considering the small size of our constructed dataset, the experimental results reported in this chapter were based on 10-fold cross-validation. In particular, we broke data into ten sets of size 318 users per set. We trained our model on nine sets and tested it on one set each time. We repeated such process ten times and took a mean accuracy as the ultimate result.

6.6.2   FEATURE EXTRACTION

Textual Features for Twitter and Foursquare

After textual data preprocessing, we extracted and normalized the following features:

- **User topics**. According to our observation, users may have higher probabilities of talking about topics related to their occupations. This motivates us to explore the topic distributions of users' social posts to characterize their occupations. For each user, we merged his/her tweets (Foursquare tips) into one document to represent the Twitter (Foursquare) source. We generated topic distributions using Latent Dirichlet Allocation (LDA [15], which has been widely found to be useful in latent topic modeling [57, 142]). Based on the metric of perplexity [69] that is frequently utilized to find the optimal number of hidden topics, we ultimately obtained 50 and 30 dimensional topic-level features over users' tweets on Twitter and tips on Foursquare, respectively.

- **Linguistic Inquiry and Word Count features (LIWC)**. LIWC is widely used to analyze the psycho-linguistic transparent lexicon. It plays an important role in predicting users' personality and careers [67]. The main component of LIWC is a directory which contains the mapping from words to 72 categories.[7] Given a document, LIWC computes the percentage of words in each category and represents it as a vector of 72 dimensions.

- **Heuristically inferred features**. Inspired by [34], we extracted some heuristically inferred features. First, we counted the number of URLs, number of hash tags, and number of user mentions, since these features are correlated with users' social network activity level and can thus indicate users' occupation types. Second, we counted the number of slang words, number of emotion words,[8] and number of emoticons and computed an average sentiment score. These features can be good signals of user personality traits, which in turn are occupation dependent. Third, we computed some writing behavior style features, including "number

---

[7]http://www.liwc.net/
[8]www.sentiwordnet.isti.cnr.it

of repeated characters" in words, "number of misspellings," and "number of unknown to the spell checker words," which are often reflected by users' occupations. In this way, we extracted 14-D features.

Semantic Location Features for Foursquare

Beside the topic features extracted from the tips, we also extracted the semantic location features for the source of Foursquare. In particular, we utilized two attributes related to the check-in behaviors. First, we collected the well-structured and hierarchically organized venue categories of Foursquare.[9] Each Foursquare venue is mapped to one or more categories depending on its social function. Second, users visit venues at different times, which shows the temporal dimensions related to users' behaviors. To explore the semantics of spatial and temporal information, we represent each user by a weighted vector, where each dimension represents a visit to a particular venue category at a particular time period. In total, we utilized 423 leaf categories and the eight different time periods, which are {morning (5am–11am), afternoon (12pm–18pm), evening (19pm–23pm), night (12am–4am)} × {weekday, weekend}.

Visual Features for Instagram

To represent the content of each image, we extracted the following features:

- **Local Features.** We used the difference of Gaussians to detect keypoints in each image and extracted their SIFT descriptors. By building a visual codebook of size 1,000 based on K-means, we obtained a 1,000-D bag-of-visual-words histogram for each image [56].

- **Global Features.** We further extracted 428-D global visual features, including 225-D block-wise color moments based on 5-by-5 fixed partition of the image; 128-D wavelet texture; and 75-D edge direction histogram [85].

In summary, we extracted 136-D, 547-D, and 1,428-D features for each given user from their Twitter, Foursquare, and Instagram sources, respectively. We fed the features into our model for validation.[10]

6.6.3 OVERALL MODEL EVALUATION

To demonstrate the effectiveness of our proposed user attributes learning model, we comparatively verified the following state-of-the-arts competitors:

- *SVM*: Support Vector Machine is a typical mono-source mono-task learning model [21]. We concatenated all the features from multiple sources into a single vector and trained each task separately. With the assist of LIBSVM,[11] we chose radial-basis as our kernel function.

---

[9]https://developer.foursquare.com/categorytree
[10]Actually, we also investigated some other possible features, such as some n-grams and part-of-speech tags, but these features do not have a strong relation with occupation inference, and hence detailed description and evaluation on such features are omitted in this book.
[11]http://www.csie.ntu.edu.tw/~cjlin/libsvm

- *GLR*: Group Lasso Regularization method [22, 81] is a $\ell_{2,1}$-norm penalty for group feature selection $\frac{1}{2}\|\mathbf{XW} - \mathbf{Y}\|_F^2 + \rho\|\mathbf{W}\|_F^2 + \sigma\|\mathbf{W}\|_{2,1}$. This model encodes the group sparsity but fails to take the task relatedness and source relatedness into account.

- *MSIF*: The authors in [49] proposed a Multi-Source Integration Framework to infer users' occupation from their social activities recorded in the social sites, which combines both content model and network model. As reported in [49], this work outperforms most of the prevailing occupation inference approaches. That is why we did not selected others as competitors.

- *MTL*: As a typical example of the traditional multi-task learning model, the work in [139] aims to automatically capture and model the task relatedness. It is formulated as $\frac{1}{2}\|\mathbf{XW} - \mathbf{Y}\|_F^2 + \upsilon\|\mathbf{W}\boldsymbol{\Omega}^{-1}\mathbf{W}^T\|_F^2 + \varrho\|\mathbf{W}\|_F^2$. The code for this model is available here.[12]

- *regMVMT*: A semi-supervised inductive multi-view multi-task learning model introduced in [136]. As reported in [136], this model regulates both the source consistency and the task relatedness. However, it simply assumes and characterizes the uniform relatedness among tasks.

- *STATUS*: Our proposed graph-guided multi-task multi-source learning model.

We can see that the selected competitors are very comprehensive, including mono-source mono-task learning, group lasso regularization, multi-task learning, multi-source learning, as well as multi-source multi-task learning. For each method mentioned above, the involved parameters were carefully tuned with 5-fold cross validation in the training data between 10^{-2} to 10^2, and the parameters with the best performance with respect to $P@5$ were used to report the final results.

The comparison results of various models for occupation inference from multiple social media sources are shown in Tables 6.3 and 6.4. Experimental results are measured by $P@K$ and $S@K$, respectively. From this table, we have some observations: (1) *SVM* achieves the worst performance. One possible reason may be the insufficient positive training samples for certain occupation titles. For instance, only 18 positive training samples are available for the occupation "musician." (2) *GLR* is slightly better than *SVM*, but still worse than others. In this model, the weights of each feature over all tasks are grouped using the ℓ_2 norm, and all features are further grouped using the ℓ_1 norm. This model thus tends to select features based on the strength of the feature over all tasks. Its result confirms that some features have little description power for all the tasks and hence feature selection is necessary. (3) *MSIF* and *MTL* show their superiors to *SVM* and *GLR*. The reason may be that they either explicitly consider the source fusion, or consider the task relatedness. Appropriate source fusion can enhance user characterization and multiple task learning can effectively increase the number of samples by learning multiple related tasks

---

[12]http://www.comp.hkbu.edu.hk/~yuzhang/codes/MTRL.zip

Table 6.3: Performance comparison among various models for occupation inference from multiple social media platforms. The performance is measured in terms of $S@K$ (%).

Approaches	S@1	S@2	S@3	S@4	S@5
SVM	41.04	56.26	66.29	72.67	75.38
GLR	46.73	60.53	69.81	75.97	77.26
MSIF	50.31	63.46	72.33	79.18	82.30
MTL	51.29	65.09	73.58	78.58	81.76
regMV MT	55.97	68.84	77.92	85.19	88.02
STATUS	**60.50**	**72.58**	**82.04**	**88.46**	**92.77**

Table 6.4: Performance comparison among various models for occupation inference from multiple social media platforms. The performance is measured in terms of $P@K$ (%).

Approaches	P@1	P@2	P@3	P@4	P@5
SVM	41.04	28.13	22.10	18.17	15.08
GLR	46.73	30.27	23.27	18.99	15.45
MSIF	50.31	31.73	24.11	19.80	16.46
MTL	51.29	32.55	24.53	19.65	16.35
regMV MT	55.97	34.42	25.97	21.30	17.60
STATUS	**60.50**	**36.29**	**27.35**	**22.11**	**18.55**

simultaneously. (4) *regMVMT* outperforms all the competitors, except *STATUS*. This is because it jointly regularizes the task relatedness and source fusion. However, it restricts the relatedness among tasks in a uniform way without considering the prior knowledge. Moreover, it is unable to select discriminative task-specific and task-sharing features. As an extension of *regMVMT*, our proposed *STATUS* has resolved these issues by leveraging graph-guided fused lasso penalty. That is why it achieves the best performance consistently in terms of $S@K$ and $P@K$ at different depths. And (5) the performance in terms of $S@1$ and $P@1$ is as high as 60.50%; that means for up to 60% users, our model can precisely infer their occupations, if our model only predicted one occupation for each user only. Meanwhile, the value of $S@5$ almost ensures that at least one occupation is correct among the top five predicted ones.

We also conducted the analysis of variance (known as ANOVA) based on $S@5$ and $P@5$, respectively. To be more specific, we performed pairwise t-test between our proposed *STATUS* model and each of the competitors based on 10-fold cross validation results in terms of $S@5$ and $P@5$. The results are summarized in Table 6.5. It can be observed that all the p-values are much smaller than 0.05, which shows that the improvements of our proposed model over other baselines are statistically significant.

Table 6.5: The p-value of pairwise significance test between our proposed *STATUS* model and each of the baselines. We can see that all the p-values are greatly smaller than 0.05, and they indicate that the differences are significant.

Pairwise Significance Test	Metrics	
	p-value over S@5	p-value over P@5
STATUS vs. *SVM*	$2.82e\text{-}05$	$1.79e\text{-}03$
STATUS vs. *GLR*	$5.32e\text{-}04$	$1.03e\text{-}03$
STATUS vs. *MSIF*	$6.80e\text{-}03$	$5.31e\text{-}02$
STATUS vs. *MTL*	$1.28e\text{-}03$	$4.08e\text{-}02$
STATUS vs. *regMV MT*	$1.05e\text{-}03$	$2.07e\text{-}02$

6.6.4 COMPONENT-WISE ANALYSIS

To examine how effective each component is in the proposed *STATUS* model, we carried out experiments to compare the performance of the following methods. In fact, these methods can be deduced from our *STATUS* model by excluding some terms:

- *SLF*: Squared Loss Function can be derived by setting λ, β, and μ to be zero, respectively. In this case, we do not consider both the source relatedness and task relatedness.

- *MSL*: Multi-Source Learning model can be obtained by setting β as zero. In such case, the graph-guided fused lasso is not considered.

- *MTLg*: Multi-Task Learning model with Graph-guided penalty is a special case of our proposed *STATUS* model by setting λ to be zero [23]. In such a context, the source relatedness is not taken into consideration.

- *STATUS*: Our proposed multi-source learning model with graph-guided fused lasso penalty.

The results of component-wise analysis are summarized in Tables 6.6 and 6.7. From this table, the following observations can be made: (1) *SLF* is the most unsatisfactory method, whose result is even worse than that of *SVM*. This may be caused by three facts. First, the model of *SLF* does not support the function of sparsity or complexity control, and hence it is easy to be overfitting. Second, it neither explores the structural relatedness among tasks, nor considers the agreement among sources. Third, it is unable to select descriptive features. The comparative results imply that feature selection, multi-source learning, and multi-task learning are of vital importance for user attributes learning. (2) The performance of *MSL* is much better than *SLF*, but it is less promising as compared to that of *MTLg*. This demonstrates that graph-guided fused lasso penalty holds more encouraging effects than that of multi-source fusion. The main reason may be that our dataset is not very large, and *MTLg* enables the training samples sharing among closely related tasks, which greatly alleviates the problem of insufficient training samples. (3) Jointly and comparatively analyzing Tables 6.3 and 6.6, Tables 6.4 and 6.7, we can see that *MTLg* performs better than the conventional *MTL*. The possible reason is that, beside task relatedness modeling, the former also plays a role in feature selection. And (4) our proposed *STATUS* seamlessly sews all these components and stably works best. We also conducted the pairwise significance test between *STATUS* and each of its components. All the p-values are smaller than 0.05, which shows that the improvements boosted by *STATUS* are statistically significant.

Table 6.6: Experimental results of component-wise analysis. The experimental results are measured by $S@K$ (%).

Components	S@1	S@2	S@3	S@4	S@5
SLF	39.53	56.79	63.27	68.05	71.04
MSL	52.67	64.06	73.84	80.72	84.91
MTLg	54.09	67.61	75.60	82.23	87.45
STATUS	**60.50**	**72.58**	**82.04**	**88.46**	**92.77**

Table 6.7: Experimental results of component-wise analysis. The experimental results are measured by $P@K$ (%).

Components	P@1	P@2	P@3	P@4	P@5
SLF	39.53	28.40	21.09	17.01	14.21
MSL	52.67	32.03	24.61	20.18	16.98
MTLg	54.09	33.81	25.20	20.56	17.49
STATUS	**60.50**	**36.29**	**27.35**	**22.11**	**18.55**

6.6.5   SOURCE INTEGRATION

We believe that the discriminative capabilities for individual source or source combinations vary significantly. We thus conducted experiments to study the representativeness of individual sources and various source combinations for user occupation inferences.

Table 6.8 comparatively displays the experimental results. Notably, when learning on individual source, our proposed *STATUS* model degenerates into a multi-task learning model with graph-guided penalty, which only considers the task relatedness and feature selection. It is intuitive that feeding our model with all the three sources obtains the best results. Meanwhile, we noticed that the model trained on individual Twitter is effectively ahead of that trained on individual Foursquare and Instagram, respectively. This reveals that the Twitter source is much more informative in the user representation. One reason for such a result may be that the users in our dataset are very active on Twitter and the data crawled from Twitter is hence very intensive. We also observed that in the bi-source combinations, the integration of Twitter and Foursquare outperforms others, but is still suboptimal as compared to the tri-source combination. This tells us that the visual information from Instagram is a positive added value. From the last column of Table 6.8, it can be seen that the model leveraging all the three sources is statistically better than those leveraging only parts of them.

Table 6.8: Experimental results of source combination evaluation. The experimental results are measured by $S@K$ and $P@K$, respectively (%). The last column displays the results of pairwise significance test between the model leveraging all the three sources and those only leveraging parts of them (based on 10-fold cross validation results in terms of $P@5$.).

Source Combination	S@1	S@3	S@5	P@1	P@3	P@5	p-value
Twitter	57.55	79.34	90.72	57.55	26.45	18.14	1.06e-02
Instagram	35.50	56.98	63.27	35.50	18.99	12.65	4.26e-06
Foursquare	41.86	62.80	70.60	41.86	20.93	14.12	3.41e-05
Twitter + Instagram	58.02	79.91	81.60	58.02	26.64	16.32	1.87e-02
Twitter + Foursquare	59.03	80.91	91.82	59.03	26.97	18.36	2.45e-02
Instagram + Foursquare	48.05	68.62	74.53	48.05	22.87	14.91	8.26e-04
Twitter + Instagram + Foursquare	**60.50**	**82.04**	**92.77**	**60.50**	**27.35**	**18.55**	—–

6.6.6   PARAMETER TUNING

Our model holds three key parameters as shown in Eq. (6.3). The optimal values of these parameters were carefully tuned with 5-fold cross-validation in the training data. In particular, based upon the 10-fold cross-validation, we have around 2,862 users during each training round. We performed 5-fold cross-validation on the 2,862 users to learn the optimal parameters by grid search strategy between 10^{-2} to 10^2 with small but adaptive step size. The step size was 0.01, 0.05, 1, and 5 for the range of $[0.01, 0.1]$, $[0.1, 1]$, $[1, 10]$, and $[10, 100]$, respectively. The parameters corresponding to the best $P@5$ were used to report the final results. For other competitors, the procedures to tune the parameters are analogous to ensure fair comparison.

6.6.7   COMPUTATIONAL ANALYSIS

In the training process, the computational complexity comes from three parts: (1) graph construction and normalization, $O(C^3)$; (2) calculation of $\mathbf{A}$ and $\mathbf{W}$, $O(D \times (C + |\mathcal{E}|))$ and $O(D^3 + CD^2)$, respectively; and (3) the alternative iteration between $\mathbf{A}$ and $\mathbf{W}$, p times. Thereinto, C, D, $|\mathcal{E}|$ and p respectively refer to the number of occupation titles studied in our work, the feature dimensions extracted from all the sources, number of edges in the constructed graph, and iteration times. Hence, the overall time complexity scales as $O(C^3 + p(D^3 + CD^2 + CD + D|\mathcal{E}|))$. Usually, D is much larger than C, and the final complexity can be thus restated as $O(pD^3)$. In our work, C is 80, D is $2, 111$, and p is in the order of hundreds. The process can be completed in less than 10 s excluding feature extraction over a computer equipped with a 3.4 GHZ CPU with 16 GB RAM. Therefore, our model has a large potential to be applied to other web-scale or realtime applications.

6.7   OTHER APPLICATION

People go to fortune tellers in hopes of learning things about their future. A future career path is one of the topics most frequently discussed. But rather than rely on "black arts" to make predictions, we can scientifically and systematically study the feasibility of career path prediction from social network data by our proposed *STATUS* model.

A user's career path refers to the user's occupational growth in his or her career life. It comprises several distinct career stages, and each stage contains a set of equivalent occupational titles. The objective of this work is to predict the future career stages of a given user, the so-called career path modeling, which can provide potential benefits for employees, employers, and headhunters. For employees, they can get information about their current career stages, the time point for their next job-hop, as well as the whole picture of their own career paths. For employers, they will be informed of the career progressions of their employees and decide what would be the best time to promote their employees or increase their salaries. When it comes to headhunters, they could be advised of the appropriate time to talk to their target customers as well as the proper job positions for their customers. These efficient and accurate job hunting and recommendation processes will greatly facilitate headhunting and reduce their efforts considerably. As a consequence, career path modeling is a research topic with high potential and has many real-world applications.

Beside the source fusion and feature selection challenges, a user's career path normally comprises a sequence of occupations. Instead of mutual independence, they are correlated with each other in chronological order. Therefore, how to temporally characterize such relatedness poses another challenge. Toward this end, we can equally split the career path into multiple time intervals, and each of them is treated as a task. A career path is generally a gradual process, and hence sudden changes of career stages between neighboring time points should be penalized. For instance, it is much more smooth for a research fellow to become an assistant professor rather than a full professor in their next position. As you can see, when applying *STATUS* to model the career path, it is different from occupation inference. Here a task is a time point for one specific career path.

The detailed information of this application can be found in this paper [75].

6.8   SUMMARY

This chapter presents a novel multi-source multi-task learning model for user attributes learning from multimodal and multimedia sources. This model seamlessly sews information cues from heterecious sources, and regularizes the inter-task relatedness with the graph-guided penalty. In addition, it also jointly learns the task-sharing and task-specific features via lasso and graph-guided fused lasso. The graph-structure is constructed by leveraging the external and internal knowledge. We relaxed the non-smooth objective function to a smooth one, and derived its optimization process. To validate our proposed model, we crawled ground truth, short texts, check-ins, and images from four prevailing sources, namely, Linkedin, Twitter, Foursquare, and Instagram. Representative features were extracted from these sources to characterize users from various views. Extensive experiments on this dataset shows the priority of our model to the baselines. It is worth mentioning that our model is flexible to incorporate more sources and it is applicable to infer other attributes beyond occupations.

CHAPTER 7

Research Frontiers

In this book we presented some application-motivated problems. To solve these problems, we introduced some general principles, methodologies, and optimizations by jointly learning from multiple social networks. In particular, we first declared an engineering approach to multi-source data gathering and theoretical methods for data completion. The task of data completion is to estimate the missing data caused by the fact that some users may be very active in certain social networks while inactive in others. We then developed a novel and robust multi-source mono-task learning model to collaboratively integrate information cues from multiple social networks, which is applied it to the application of volunteerism tendency prediction. Following that, an efficient mono-source multi-task learning model was designed to handle multi-class problems, which was validated on the application of user interest inference. After that, we generalized the above two models to a series of multi-source multi-task learning models, and demonstrated the effectiveness of these models on practical applications, such as occupation prediction.

That being said, learning from multiple social networks is still a young and highly promising research field. There are many unexplored but fruitful future directions and challenging research issues. We illustrate a few of them here.

Complementary Relatedness

The philosophy behind the multi-source learning models covered in this book is source agreement. In other words, the predicted results from individual sources should be equal or very close to each other, and the differences are penalized by regularizations. But we ignore another important relatedness among sources, i.e., complementarity. Complementarity is defined as the information revealed by source A cannot be replaced by or inferred from source B. The use of the complementary relatedness among resources can create additional, super-additive value synergies that are not captured by source consistency.

Besides, the complementary part of a specific source is not necessarily useful for all the desired tasks. Take user occupation inference as an example. Assume that we are given a set of users and their two sources comprising of Quora and Facebook. Each user is associated with one occupation (task) of programmer, doctor, cook. As known, well-educated professionals prefer answering questions in Quora. Hence, the complementary part on Quora is useful for the task of programmer and doctor, but not cook. In comparison, cook may often share their photos on Facebook. Thus, the complementary part on Facebook is beneficial to the task of cook. We need to preserve the useful cues and keep out the useless ones. How to identify the task-specific useful knowledge from complementary part in each source remains largely an unaddressed research problem.

Privacy Issues in Multi-sources

Due to the public nature of online social networks, privacy is a significant issue, as people are likely to share their daily lives online. According to the report [99], 50% of Internet users were concerned with the information disclosed about them online, which was about 30% in 2009. Privacy is defined as the individual's ability to control what information is disclosed, to whom, when, and under what circumstances [9]. Several efforts have been dedicated to this growing research area [64], such as re-identification [7, 42], data publishing [144], and differential privacy [31]. However, most of the existing work focus on a single social network. In reality, users can leak their private daily life on Twitter, personal identifier attributes on Facebook, and their employer on LinkedIn, aggregating these users' information leakages from multiple social networks is a promising research area [38, 40]. Furthermore, to the best of our knowledge, very limited work regarding privacy has been done on UGCs from the perspective of content analysis, which is the most challenging and of great value.

Investigating the privacy issue across multiple social networks, however, is non-trivial due to the following reasons. First, how to characterize and model privacy is a tough challenge. The interpretation of privacy may be subjective and differs from individuals to individuals. In such situations, some guidelines should be predefined, which declare what information is private and the privacy degree. Apart from investigating the literature of social science, user study may be helpful to obtain such relevant guideline. Second, some prescriptive analysis should be given to help users protect their privacy. Once we detect that some information is leaked by UGCs, what kinds of actions can be done to relieve the affects? Last but not least, due to the freedom and limited-length nature of UGCs, the noisy data would hinder the effective content analysis.

Bibliography

[1] F. Abel, E. Herder, G.-J. Houben, N. Henze, and D. Krause. Cross-system user modeling and personalization on the social web. *User Modeling and User-Adapted Interaction*, 23(2–3), pages 169–209, 2013. DOI: 10.1007/s11257-012-9131-2. 7, 18, 42, 50

[2] F. Abel, E. Herder, and D. Krause. Extraction of professional interests from social web profiles. In *Workshop on Augmenting User Models with Real World Experiences to Enhance Personalization and Adaptation*, 2011. 50

[3] S. Adali and J. Golbeck. Predicting personality with social behavior. In *IEEE/ACM International Conference on Advances in Social Networks Analysis and Mining*, pages 302–309, 2012. DOI: 10.1109/asonam.2012.58. 19

[4] A. Argyriou, S. Clémençon, and R. Zhang. Learning the graph of relations among multiple tasks. *Research Report*, 2013. 36

[5] A. Argyriou, T. Evgeniou, and M. Pontil. Multi-task feature learning. In *Advances in Neural Information Processing Systems*, pages 41–48. MIT Press, 2006. 45

[6] A. Argyriou, T. Evgeniou, and M. Pontil. Convex multi-task feature learning. *Machine Learning*, 73, pages 243–272, 2008. DOI: 10.1007/s10994-007-5040-8. 45, 53

[7] L. Backstrom, C. Dwork, and J. Kleinberg. Wherefore art thou r3579x?: Anonymized social networks, hidden patterns, and structural steganography. In *Proc. of the International Conference on World Wide Web*, pages 181–190. ACM, 2007. DOI: 10.1145/1242572.1242598. 86

[8] S. Bai, T. Zhu, and L. Cheng. Big-five personality prediction based on user behaviors at social network sites. *arXiv:1204.4809*, 2012. 19

[9] S. B. Barnes. A privacy paradox: Social networking in the united states. *First Monday*, 11, 2006. DOI: 10.5210/fm.v11i9.1394. 86

[10] M. R. Barrick and M. K. Mount. The big five personality dimensions and job performance: A meta-analysis. 44, pages 1–26, 1991. DOI: 10.1111/j.1744-6570.1991.tb00688.x. 19

[11] B. Bazelli, A. Hindle, and E. Stroulia. On the personality traits of stackoverflow users. In *IEEE International Conference on Software Maintenance*, pages 460–463, 2013. DOI: 10.1109/icsm.2013.72. 19, 27

[12] F. Benevenuto, T. Rodrigues, V. Almeida, J. Almeida, and M. Gonçalves. Detecting spammers and content promoters in online video social networks. In *Proc. of the International ACM SIGIR Conference on Research and Development in Information Retrieval*, pages 620–627, 2009. DOI: 10.1145/1571941.1572047. 28

[13] P. Bhattacharya, M. B. Zafar, N. Ganguly, S. Ghosh, and K. P. Gummadi. Inferring user interests in the twitter social network. In *Proc. of the ACM Conference on Recommender systems*, RecSys, pages 357–360, 2014. DOI: 10.1145/2645710.2645765. 37

[14] B. Bi, M. Shokouhi, M. Kosinski, and T. Graepel. Inferring the demographics of search users: Social data meets search queries. In *Proc. of the International Conference on World Wide Web*, pages 131–140. International World Wide Web Conferences Steering Committee, 2013. DOI: 10.1145/2488388.2488401. 65

[15] D. M. Blei, A. Y. Ng, and M. I. Jordan. Latent dirichlet allocation. In *The Journal of Machine Learning Research*, 3, pages 993–1022, 2003. 27, 43, 75

[16] S. Bordag. A comparison of co-occurrence and similarity measures as simulations of context. In *Proc. of the International Conference on Computational Linguistics and Intelligent Text Processing*, pages 52–63. Springer-Verlag, 2008. DOI: 10.1007/978-3-540-78135-6_5. 57

[17] J. D. Burger, J. Henderson, G. Kim, and G. Zarrella. Discriminating gender on twitter. In *Proc. of the Conference on Empirical Methods in Natural Language Processing*, pages 1301–1309. Association for Computational Linguistics, 2011. 65

[18] G. Carlo, M. A. Okun, G. P. Knight, and M. R. T. de Guzman. The interplay of traits and motives on volunteering: agreeableness, extraversion and prosocial value motivation. *Personality and Individual Differences*, 38, pages 1293–1305, 2005. DOI: 10.1016/j.paid.2004.08.012. 19, 20

[19] D. Carmel, N. Zwerdling, I. Guy, S. Ofek-Koifman, N. Har'el, I. Ronen, E. Uziel, S. Yogev, and S. Chernov. Personalized social search based on the user's social network. In *Proc. of the ACM Conference on Information and Knowledge Management*, pages 1227–1236, 2009. DOI: 10.1145/1645953.1646109. 18

[20] Z. Cemalcilar. Understanding individual characteristics of adolescents who volunteer. *Personality and Individual Differences*, 46, pages 432–436, 2009. DOI: 10.1016/j.paid.2008.11.009. 19

[21] C.-C. Chang and C.-J. Lin. Libsvm: A library for support vector machines. *ACM Transactions on Intelligent Systems and Technology*, 2:27:1–27:27, 2011. DOI: 10.1145/1961189.1961199. 29, 58, 76

[22] O. Chapelle, E. Manavoglu, and R. Rosales. Simple and scalable response prediction for display advertising. *ACM Transactions on Intelligent Systems and Technology*, 5:61:1–61:34, 2014. DOI: 10.1145/2532128. 77

[23] X. Chen, S. Kim, Q. Lin, J. G. Carbonell, and E. P. Xing. Graph-structured multi-task regression and an efficient optimization method for general fused lasso. *Computing Research Repository*, 2010. 79

[24] P. Cimiano, A. Schultz, S. Sizov, P. Sorg, and S. Staab. Explicit versus latent concept models for cross-language information retrieval. In *Proc. of the International Joint Conference on Artifical Intelligence*, pages 1513–1518. Morgan Kaufmann Publishers Inc., 2009. 43

[25] M. Claypool, D. Brown, P. Le, and M. Waseda. Inferring user interest. *IEEE Internet Computing*, 5, pages 32–39, 2001. DOI: 10.1109/4236.968829. 37

[26] M. Conover, J. Ratkiewicz, M. Francisco, B. Gonçalves, A. Flammini, and F. Menczer. Political polarization on twitter. In *Proc. of the International AAAI Conference on Weblogs and Social Media*, The AAAI Press, 2011. 65

[27] C. Cortes and V. Vapnik. Support-vector networks. *Machine Learning*, 20, pages 273–297, 1995. DOI: 10.1007/BF00994018. 58

[28] M. H. Davis, K. V. Mitchell, J. A. Hall, J. Lothert, T. Snapp, and M. Meyer. Empathy, expectations, and situational preferences: Personality influences on the decision to participate in volunteer helping behaviors. *Journal of Personality*, 67, pages 469–503, 1999. DOI: 10.1111/1467-6494.00062. 19

[29] M. De Choudhury, M. Gamon, S. Counts, and E. Horvitz. Predicting depression via social media. In *The International Conference on Weblogs and Social Media*, AAAI, 2013. 65

[30] Y. Dong, Y. Yang, J. Tang, Y. Yang, and N. V. Chawla. Inferring user demographics and social strategies in mobile social networks. In *Proc. of the ACM SIGKDD International Conference on Knowledge Discovery and Data Mining*, pages 15–24, 2014. DOI: 10.1145/2623330.2623703. 65

[31] C. Dwork, F. McSherry, K. Nissim, and A. Smith. Calibrating noise to sensitivity in private data analysis. In *Proc. of the Conference on Theory of Cryptography*, pages 265–284. Springer-Verlag, 2006. DOI: 10.1007/11681878_14. 86

[32] C. A. Eldering. Advertisement selection system supporting discretionary target market characteristics, 2001. U.S. Patent 6,216,129. 35

[33] F. F. Faria, A. Veloso, H. M. Almeida, E. Valle, R. d. S. Torres, M. A. Gonçalves, and W. Meira, Jr. Learning to rank for content-based image retrieval. In *Proc. of the International Conference on Multimedia Information Retrieval*, pages 285–294. ACM, 2010. DOI: 10.1145/1743384.1743434. 3

[34] A. Farseev, L. Nie, M. Akbari, and T.-S. Chua. Harvesting multiple sources for user profile learning: a big data study. In *Proc. of the ACM on International Conference on Multimedia Retrieval*, pages 235–242, 2015. DOI: 10.1145/2671188.2749381. 75

[35] H. Fei and J. Huan. Structured feature selection and task relationship inference for multi-task learning. In *IEEE International Conference on Data Mining*, pages 171–180, 2011. DOI: 10.1109/icdm.2011.139. 49

[36] H. Fei, R. Jiang, Y. Yang, B. Luo, and J. Huan. Content based social behavior prediction: A multi-task learning approach. In *Proc. of the ACM International Conference on Information and Knowledge Management*, pages 995–1000, 2011. DOI: 10.1145/2063576.2063719. 37

[37] Y. Gao, M. Wang, Z.-J. Zha, J. Shen, X. Li, and X. Wu. Visual-textual joint relevance learning for tag-based social image search. *IEEE Transactions on Image Processing*, 22, pages 363–376, 2013. DOI: 10.1109/tip.2012.2202676. 24

[38] O. Goga, H. Lei, S. H. K. Parthasarathi, G. Friedland, R. Sommer, and R. Teixeira. Exploiting innocuous activity for correlating users across sites. In *Proc. of the International Conference on World Wide Web*, pages 447–458. International World Wide Web Conferences Steering Committee, 2013. DOI: 10.1145/2488388.2488428. 86

[39] O. Goga, P. Loiseau, R. Sommer, R. Teixeira, and K. P. Gummadi. On the reliability of profile matching across large online social networks. In *Proc. of the ACM SIGKDD International Conference on Knowledge Discovery and Data Mining*, pages 1799–1808, 2015. DOI: 10.1145/2783258.2788601. 7

[40] O. Goga, P. Loiseau, R. Sommer, R. Teixeira, and K. P. Gummadi. On the reliability of profile matching across large online social networks. In *Proc. of the ACM SIGKDD International Conference on Knowledge Discovery and Data Mining*, pages 1799–1808, 2015. DOI: 10.1145/2783258.2788601. 86

[41] L. Gou, M. X. Zhou, and H. Yang. Knowme and shareme: Understanding automatically discovered personality traits from social media and user sharing preferences. In *Proc. of the Annual ACM Conference on Human Factors in Computing Systems*, CHI, pages 955–964, 2014. DOI: 10.1145/2556288.2557398. 65

[42] R. Gross and A. Acquisti. Information revelation and privacy in online social networks. In *Proc. of the ACM Workshop on Privacy in the Electronic Society*, pages 71–80, 2005. DOI: 10.1145/1102199.1102214. 86

[43] J. Guo, G. Xu, X. Cheng, and H. Li. Named entity recognition in query. In *Proc. of the International ACM SIGIR Conference on Research and Development in Information Retrieval*, pages 267–274, 2009. DOI: 10.1145/1571941.1571989. 27

[44] I. Guy, U. Avraham, D. Carmel, S. Ur, M. Jacovi, and I. Ronen. Mining expertise and interests from social media. In *Proc. of the International Conference on World Wide Web*, pages 515–526. International World Wide Web Conferences Steering Committee, 2013. DOI: 10.1145/2488388.2488434. 37

[45] L. Han, Y. Zhang, G. Song, and K. Xie. Encoding tree sparsity in multi-task learning: A probabilistic framework. In *Proc. of the AAAI Conference on Artificial Intelligence*, pages 1854–1860. AAAI Press, 2014. 36

[46] J. He and R. Lawrence. A graph-based framework for multi-task multi-view learning. In *Proc. of the International Conference on Machine Learning*, pages 25–32. Omnipress, 2011. 50, 65

[47] J. Hitchen. *Implementing a Volunteer–Match Service*. Ph.D. thesis, Al Akhawayn University, 2013. 19

[48] C.-J. Hsieh and I. S. Dhillon. Fast coordinate descent methods with variable selection for non-negative matrix factorization. In *Proc. of the ACM SIGKDD International Conference on Knowledge Discovery and Data Mining*, pages 1064–1072, 2011. DOI: 10.1145/2020408.2020577. 15

[49] Y. Huang, L. Yu, X. Wang, and B. Cui. A multi-source integration framework for user occupation inference in social media systems. *World Wide Web*, 18, pages 1247–1267, 2015. DOI: 10.1007/s11280-014-0300-6. 77

[50] F. Iacobelli, A. J. Gill, S. Nowson, and J. Oberlander. Large scale personality classification of bloggers. In *Proc. of the International Conference on Affective Computing and Intelligent Interaction—Volume Part II*, pages 568–577. Springer-Verlag, 2011. DOI: 10.1007/978-3-642-24571-8_71. 19

[51] T. Iofciu, P. Fankhauser, F. Abel, and K. Bischoff. Identifying users across social tagging systems. In *International Conference on Weblogs and Social Media*. The AAAI Press, 2011. 7

[52] T. Iwata, S. Watanabe, T. Yamada, and N. Ueda. Topic tracking model for analyzing consumer purchase behavior. In *Proc. of the International Joint Conference on Artifical Intelligence*, pages 1427–1432. Morgan Kaufmann Publishers Inc., 2009. 43

[53] L. Jacob, J.-p. Vert, and F. R. Bach. Clustered multi-task learning: A convex formulation. In *Advances in Neural Information Processing Systems*, pages 745–752. MIT Press, 2009. 37

[54] J. Jeon, V. Lavrenko, and R. Manmatha. Automatic image annotation and retrieval using cross-media relevance models. In *Proc. of the 26th Annual International ACM SIGIR Conference on Research and Development in Informaion Retrieval*, pages 119–126, 2003. DOI: 10.1145/860435.860459. 3

[55] R. Ji, L.-Y. Duan, J. Chen, T. Huang, and W. Gao. Mining compact bag-of-patterns for low bit rate mobile visual search. *IEEE Transactions on Image Processing*, 23, pages 3099–3113, 2014. DOI: 10.1109/tip.2014.2324291. 63

[56] R. Ji, L.-Y. Duan, J. Chen, L. Xie, H. Yao, and W. Gao. Learning to distribute vocabulary indexing for scalable visual search. *IEEE Transactions on Multimedia*, 15, pages 153–166, 2013. DOI: 10.1109/tmm.2012.2225035. 76

[57] R. Ji, Y. Gao, W. Liu, X. Xie, Q. Tian, and X. Li. When location meets social multimedia: A survey on vision-based recognition and mining for geo-social multimedia analytics. *ACM Transactions on Intelligent Systems and Technology*, 6:1:1–1:18, 2015. DOI: 10.1145/2597181. 75

[58] X. Jin, F. Zhuang, S. Wang, Q. He, and Z. Shi. Shared structure learning for multiple tasks with multiple views. In *Machine Learning and Knowledge Discovery in Databases*, vol. 8189, pages 353–368, 2013. DOI: 10.1007/978-3-642-40991-2_23. 51

[59] S. Kim, K. Koh, M. Lustig, S. Boyd, and D. Gorinevsky. A method for large-scale l1-regularized least squares problems with applications in signal processing and statistics. *Journal of Selected Topics in Signal Processing*, 2007. 29, 58

[60] S. Kim and E. P. Xing. Tree-guided group lasso for multi-task regression with structured sparsity. In *Proc. of the International Conference on Machine Learning*, pages 543–550, 2010. DOI: 10.1214/12-aoas549. 36, 55

[61] C. Kohlschütter, P. Fankhauser, and W. Nejdl. Boilerplate detection using shallow text features. In *Proc. of the ACM International Conference on Web Search and Data Mining*, pages 441–450, 2010. DOI: 10.1145/1718487.1718542. 53, 56

[62] Y. Konig, R. Twersky, and M. R. Berthold. Automatic, personalized online information and product services, 2005. U.S. Patent 6,981,040. 35

[63] N. Korula and S. Lattanzi. An efficient reconciliation algorithm for social networks. In *Proc. of the VLDB Endowment*, 7(5), pages 377–388, 2014. DOI: 10.14778/2732269.2732274. 7

[64] B. Krishnamurthy and C. E. Wills. On the leakage of personally identifiable information via online social networks. In *Proc. of the ACM Workshop on Online Social Networks*, pages 7–12, 2009. DOI: 10.1145/1592665.1592668. 86

[65] D. D. Lee and H. S. Seung. Algorithms for non-negative matrix factorization. In *Advances in Neural Information Processing Systems*, pages 556–562. MIT Press, 2001. 10

[66] K. Lee, J. Caverlee, and S. Webb. Uncovering social spammers: Social honeypots + machine learning. In *Proc. of the International ACM SIGIR Conference on Research and Development in Information Retrieval*, pages 435–442, 2010. DOI: 10.1145/1835449.1835522. 28

[67] K. Lee, J. Mahmud, J. Chen, M. Zhou, and J. Nichols. Who will retweet this? detecting strangers from twitter to retweet information. *ACM Transactions on Intelligent Systems and Technology*, 6:31:1–31:25, 2015. DOI: 10.1145/2700466. 75

[68] Y. Lee, S. Krishnamoorthy, and D. Dinakarpandian. A semantic framework for intelligent matchmaking for clinical trial eligibility criteria. *ACM Transactions on Intelligent Systems and Technology*, 4:71:1–71:32, 2013. DOI: 10.1145/2508037.2508052. 71

[69] D. Li, B. He, Y. Ding, J. Tang, C. Sugimoto, Z. Qin, E. Yan, J. Li, and T. Dong. Community-based topic modeling for social tagging. In *Proc. of the ACM International Conference on Information and Knowledge Management*, pages 1565–1568, 2010. DOI: 10.1145/1871437.1871673. 27, 43, 75

[70] S. Li, Y. Jiang, and Z. Zhou. Partial multi-view clustering. In *Proc. of the AAAI Conference on Artificial Intelligence*, pages 1968–1974. AAAI Press, 2014. 12, 13, 14

[71] B. Liu, Y. Fu, Z. Yao, and H. Xiong. Learning geographical preferences for point-of-interest recommendation. In *Proc. of the 19th ACM SIGKDD International Conference on Knowledge Discovery and Data Mining*, pages 1043–1051, 2013. DOI: 10.1145/2487575.2487673. 37

[72] J. Liu, F. Zhang, X. Song, Y.-I. Song, C.-Y. Lin, and H.-W. Hon. What's in a name?: An unsupervised approach to link users across communities. In *Proc. of the ACM International Conference on Web Search and Data Mining*, pages 495–504, 2013. DOI: 10.1145/2433396.2433457. 7

[73] S. Liu, S. Wang, F. Zhu, J. Zhang, and R. Krishnan. Hydra: Large-scale social identity linkage via heterogeneous behavior modeling. In *Proc. of the ACM SIGMOD International Conference on Management of Data*, pages 51–62, 2014. DOI: 10.1145/2588555.2588559. 7

[74] Y. Liu, L. Nie, L. Han, L. Zhang, and D. S. Rosenblum. Action2activity: Recognizing complex activities from sensor data. In *Proc. of the International Joint Conference on Artificial Intelligence*, pages 1617–1623. AAAI Press, 2015. 36

[75] Y. Liu, L. Zhang, L. Nie, Y. Yan, and D. S. Rosenblum. Fortune teller: Predicting your career path. In *Proc. of the AAAI Conference on Artificial Intelligence*, AAAI Press, 2016. 83

[76] H. Ma, D. Zhou, C. Liu, M. R. Lyu, and I. King. Recommender systems with social regularization. In *Proc. of the ACM International Conference on Web Search and Data Mining*, pages 287–296, 2011. DOI: 10.1145/1935826.1935877. 10

[77] Z. Ma, Y. Yang, F. Nie, J. Uijlings, and N. Sebe. Exploiting the entire feature space with sparsity for automatic image annotation. In *Proc. of the ACM International Conference on Multimedia*, pages 283–292, 2011. DOI: 10.1145/2072298.2072336. 74

[78] A. Malhotra, L. Totti, W. Meira Jr., P. Kumaraguru, and V. Almeida. Studying user footprints in different online social networks. In *Proc. of the International Conference on Advances in Social Networks Analysis and Mining (ASONAM 2012)*, pages 1065–1070. IEEE Computer Society, 2012. DOI: 10.1109/asonam.2012.184. 7

[79] D. Markovikj, S. Gievska, M. Kosinski, and D. Stillwell. Mining facebook data for predictive personality modeling. In *The International Conference on Weblogs and Social Media*, 2013. 19, 27

[80] R. R. McCrae and O. P. John. An introduction to the five-factor model and its applications. *Journal of Personality*, 60, pages 175–215, 1992. DOI: 10.1111/j.1467-6494.1992.tb00970.x. 19

[81] L. Meier, S. van de Geer, and P. Bühlmann. The group lasso for logistic regression. *Journal of the Royal Statistical Society. Series B*, 70, pages 53–71, 2008. DOI: 10.1111/j.1467-9868.2007.00627.x. 77

[82] T. M. Mitchell. *Machine Learning*. McGraw-Hill, Inc., 1997. 56

[83] M.-T. Nguyen and E.-P. Lim. On predicting religion labels in microblogging networks. In *Proc. of the International ACM SIGIR Conference on Research & Development in Information Retrieval*, pages 1211–1214. ACM, 2014. DOI: 10.1145/2600428.2609547. 65

[84] L. Nie, M. Wang, Z. Zha, G. Li, and T.-S. Chua. Multimedia answering: Enriching text qa with media information. In *Proc. of the International ACM SIGIR Conference on Research and Development in Information Retrieval*, pages 695–704, 2011. DOI: 10.1145/2009916.2010010. 9

[85] L. Nie, S. Yan, M. Wang, R. Hong, and T.-S. Chua. Harvesting visual concepts for image search with complex queries. In *Proc. of the ACM International Conference on Multimedia*, pages 59–68, 2012. DOI: 10.1145/2393347.2393363. 76

[86] L. Nie, Y.-L. Zhao, X. Wang, J. Shen, and T.-S. Chua. Learning to recommend descriptive tags for questions in social forums. *ACM Transactions on Information Systems*, 32:5:1–5:23, 2014. DOI: 10.1145/2559157. 24, 44

[87] N. Nori, D. Bollegala, and M. Ishizuka. Exploiting user interest on social media for aggregating diverse data and predicting interest. In *Proc. of the AAAI Conference on Artificial Intelligence*, pages 241–248. AAAI Press, 2011. 37

[88] C. Oh and O. Sheng. Investigating predictive power of stock micro blog sentiment in forecasting future stock price directional movement. In *International Conference on Information Systems*. Association for Information Systems, 2011. 17

[89] J. Otterbacher. Inferring gender of movie reviewers: Exploiting writing style, content and metadata. In *Proc. of the ACM International Conference on Information and Knowledge Management*, pages 369–378, 2010. DOI: 10.1145/1871437.1871487. 65

[90] M. Pennacchiotti and A.-M. Popescu. Democrats, republicans and starbucks aficionados: User classification in twitter. In *Proc. of the ACM SIGKDD International Conference on Knowledge Discovery and Data Mining*, pages 430–438, 2011. DOI: 10.1145/2020408.2020477. 29, 65

[91] M. Pennacchiotti and A.-M. Popescu. A machine learning approach to twitter user classification. In *Proc. of the International AAAI Conference on Weblogs and Social Media*. The AAAI Press, 2011. 49, 65

[92] J. W. Pennebaker and L. A. King. Linguistic styles: language use as an individual difference. In *Journal of Personality and Social Psychology*, 77, pages 1296–1312, 1999. DOI: 10.1037/0022-3514.77.6.1296. 19

[93] L. A. Penner. Dispositional and organizational influences on sustained volunteerism: An interactionist perspective. In *Journal of Social Issues*, pages 58:447–58:467, 2002. DOI: 10.1111/1540-4560.00270. 17

[94] L. A. Penner. Volunteerism and social problems: Making things better or worse? In *Journal of Social Issues*, 60, pages 645–666, 2004. DOI: 10.1111/j.0022-4537.2004.00377.x. 17, 19, 20, 27

[95] A. Popescu and G. Grefenstette. Mining user home location and gender from flickr tags. In *The International Conference on Weblogs and Social Media*. The AAAI Press, 2010. 17, 65

[96] D. Preotiuc-Pietro, V. Lampos, and N. Aletras. An analysis of the user occupational class through twitter content. In *Proc. of the Annual Meeting of the Association for Computational Linguistics and the International Joint Conference on Natural Language Processing of the Asian*

Federation of Natural Language Processing, pages 1754–1764, 2015. DOI: 10.3115/v1/p15-1169. 65

[97] D. Quercia, M. Kosinski, D. Stillwell, and J. Crowcroft. Our twitter profiles, our selves: Predicting personality with twitter. In *IEEE Inernational Conference on Social Computing Privacy, Security, Risk and Trust (PASSAT)*, pages 180–185, 2011. DOI: 10.1109/passat/socialcom.2011.26. 18

[98] D. Quercia, R. Lambiotte, D. Stillwell, M. Kosinski, and J. Crowcroft. The personality of popular facebook users. In *Proc. of the ACM Conference on Computer Supported Cooperative Work*, pages 955–964, 2012. DOI: 10.1145/2145204.2145346. 17, 18, 19

[99] L. Rainie, S. Kiesler, R. Kang, M. Madden, M. Duggan, S. Brown, and L. Dabbish. Anonymity, privacy, and security online. *Pew Research Center*, 2013. 86

[100] D. Rao, D. Yarowsky, A. Shreevats, and M. Gupta. Classifying latent user attributes in twitter. In *Proc. of the International Workshop on Search and Mining User-generated Contents*, pages 37–44, 2010. DOI: 10.1145/1871985.1871993. 65

[101] R. J. Renes. Sustained volunteerism: justification, motivation and management. 2005. 17

[102] S. Rosenthal and K. McKeown. Age prediction in blogs: A study of style, content, and online behavior in pre- and post-social media generations. In *Proc. of the Annual Meeting of the Association for Computational Linguistics: Human Language Technologies - Volume 1*, pages 763–772. Association for Computational Linguistics, 2011. 65

[103] G. Salton and M. J. McGill. *Introduction to Modern Information Retrieval*. McGraw-Hill, Inc., 1986. 56

[104] A. I. Schein, A. Popescul, L. H. Ungar, and D. M. Pennock. Methods and metrics for cold-start recommendations. In *Proc. of the Annual International ACM SIGIR Conference on Research and Development in Information Retrieval*, pages 253–260, 2002. DOI: 10.1145/564376.564421. 9, 35

[105] V. Schickel-Zuber and B. Faltings. Using hierarchical clustering for learning theontologies used in recommendation systems. In *Proc. of the ACM SIGKDD International Conference on Knowledge Discovery and Data Mining*, pages 599–608, 2007. DOI: 10.1145/1281192.1281257. 52

[106] H. A. Schwartz, J. C. Eichstaedt, M. L. Kern, L. Dziurzynski, S. M. Ramones, M. Agrawal, A. Shah, M. Kosinski, D. Stillwell, M. E. Seligman, et al. Personality, gender, and age in the language of social media: the open-vocabulary approach. *PloS one*, 2013. DOI: 10.1371/journal.pone.0073791. 19

[107] D. Sheldon. Graphical multi-task learning. In *NIPS Workshop on Structured Input—Structured Output*, 2008. 36

[108] X. Shen, B. Tan, and C. Zhai. Implicit user modeling for personalized search. In *Proc. of the ACM International Conference on Information and Knowledge Management*, pages 824–831, 2005. DOI: 10.1145/1099554.1099747. 18

[109] V. Shute and B. Towle. Adaptive e-learning. *Educational Psychologist*, 38, pages 105–114, 2003. DOI: 10.1207/s15326985ep3802_5. 35

[110] C. G. M. Snoek, M. Worring, and A. W. M. Smeulders. Early vs. late fusion in semantic video analysis. In *Proc. of the 13th Annual ACM International Conference on Multimedia*, pages 399–402, 2005. DOI: 10.1145/1101149.1101236. 3

[111] X. Song. Enrichment of user profiles across multiple online social networks for volunteerism matching for social enterprise. In *Proc. of the International ACM SIGIR Conference on Research & Development in Information Retrieval*, pages 1282–1282, 2014. DOI: 10.1145/2600428.2610383. 37

[112] X. Song, L. Nie, L. Zhang, M. Akbari, and T.-S. Chua. Multiple social network learning and its application in volunteerism tendency prediction. In *Proc. of the International ACM SIGIR Conference on Research and Development in Information Retrieval*, pages 213–222, 2015. DOI: 10.1145/2766462.2767726. 17, 74

[113] X. Song, L. Nie, L. Zhang, M. Liu, and T.-S. Chua. Interest inference via structure-constrained multi-source multi-task learning. In *Proc. of the International Conference on Artificial Intelligence*, pages 2371–2377. AAAI Press, 2015. 37, 65, 74

[114] S. Tan, Z. Guan, D. Cai, X. Qin, J. Bu, and C. Chen. Mapping users across networks by manifold alignment on hypergraph. In *Proc. of the AAAI Conference on Artificial Intelligence*, pages 159–165. AAAI Press, 2014. 7

[115] R. Tibshirani. Regression shrinkage and selection via the lasso. In *Journal of the Royal Statistical Society*, 58, pages 267–288. DOI: 10.1111/j.1467-9868.2011.00771.x. 45, 52

[116] J. Vosecky, D. Hong, and V. Shen. User identification across multiple social networks. In *International Conference on Networked Digital Technologies*, pages 360–365, 2009. DOI: 10.1109/ndt.2009.5272173. 7

[117] C. Wang, L. Zhang, and H.-J. Zhang. Learning to reduce the semantic gap in web image retrieval and annotation. In *Proc. of the 31st Annual International ACM SIGIR Conference on Research and Development in Information Retrieval*, pages 355–362, 2008. DOI: 10.1145/1390334.1390396. 3

[118] T. Wang, H. Liu, J. He, and X. Du.   Mining user interests from information sharing behaviors in social media. In *Advances in Knowledge Discovery and Data Mining*, volume 7819 of *Lecture Notes in Computer Science*, pages 85–98, 2013. DOI: 10.1007/978-3-642-37456-2_8. 37

[119] J. Warburton and T. Crosier. Are we too busy to volunteer? the relationship between time and volunteering using the 1997 abs time use data. *Australian Journal of Social Issues*, 36, pages 295–314, 2001. 17, 19

[120] X. Wei and W. B. Croft. Lda-based document models for ad-hoc retrieval. In *Proc. of the Annual International ACM SIGIR Conference on Research and Development in Information Retrieval*, pages 178–185, 2006. DOI: 10.1145/1148170.1148204. 27

[121] S. White and P. Smyth. *A Spectral Clustering Approach To Finding Communities in Graphs*, chapter 25, pages 274–285. DOI: 10.1137/1.9781611972757.25. 38

[122] W. W. Wymer Jr and S. Samu.   Volunteer service as symbolic consumption: gender and occupational differences in volunteering. In *Journal of Marketing Management*, 18, pages 971–989, 2002. DOI: 10.1362/0267257012930358. 17, 19

[123] S. Xiang, L. Yuan, W. Fan, Y. Wang, P. M. Thompson, and J. Ye. Multi-source learning with block-wise missing data for alzheimer's disease prediction. In *Proc. of the ACM SIGKDD International Conference on Knowledge Discovery and Data Mining*, pages 185–193, 2013. DOI: 10.1145/2487575.2487594. 20, 29

[124] Q. Xu, Q. Huang, and Y. Yao. Online crowdsourcing subjective image quality assessment. In *Proc. of the ACM International Conference on Multimedia*, pages 359–368, 2012. DOI: 10.1145/2393347.2393400. 70

[125] Y. Xue, X. Liao, L. Carin, and B. Krishnapuram. Multi-task learning for classification with dirichlet process priors. In *The Journal of Machine Learning Research*, 8, pages 35–63, 2007. 49

[126] T. Yarkoni. Personality in 100,000 words: a large-scale analysis of personality and word use among bloggers. In *Journal of Research in Personality*, 44, pages 363–373, 2010. DOI: 10.1016/j.jrp.2010.04.001. 19

[127] G. Ye, D. Liu, I.-H. Jhuo, and S.-F. Chang. Robust late fusion with rank minimization. In *IEEE Conference on Computer Vision and Pattern Recognition*, pages 3021–3028, 2012. DOI: 10.1109/cvpr.2012.6248032. 3, 4

[128] H. Yin, B. Cui, L. Chen, Z. Hu, and X. Zhou.   Dynamic user modeling in social media systems. *ACM Transactions on Information Systems*, 33:10:1–10:44, 2015. DOI: 10.1145/2699670. 37

[129] L. Yuan, Y. Wang, P. M. Thompson, V. A. Narayan, and J. Ye. Multi-source learning for joint analysis of incomplete multi-modality neuroimaging data. In *Proc. of the ACM SIGKDD International Conference on Knowledge Discovery and Data Mining*, pages 1149–1157, 2012. DOI: 10.1145/2339530.2339710. 9, 20

[130] X.-T. Yuan, X. Liu, and S. Yan. Visual classification with multitask joint sparse representation. In *IEEE Conference on Computer Vision and Pattern Recognition*, pages 3493–3500, 2010. DOI: 10.1109/cvpr.2010.5539967. 37

[131] R. Zafarani and H. Liu. Connecting corresponding identities across communities. In *International Conference on Weblogs and Social Media*. The AAAI Press, 2009. 7

[132] R. Zafarani and H. Liu. Connecting users across social media sites: A behavioral-modeling approach. In *Proc. of the ACM SIGKDD International Conference on Knowledge Discovery and Data Mining*, pages 41–49, 2013. DOI: 10.1145/2487575.2487648. 7

[133] F. A. Zamal, W. Liu, and D. Ruths. Homophily and latent attribute inference: Inferring latent attributes of twitter users from neighbors. In *Proc. of the International AAAI Conference on Weblogs and Social Media*, The AAAI Press, 2012. 65

[134] D. Zhai, H. Chang, S. Shan, X. Chen, and W. Gao. Multiview metric learning with global consistency and local smoothness. *ACM Transactions on Intelligent Systems and Technology*, 3:53:1–53:22, 2012. DOI: 10.1145/2168752.2168767. 33

[135] H. Zhang, M.-Y. Kan, Y. Liu, and S. Ma. Online social network profile linkage. In *Information Retrieval Technology*, volume 8870 of *Lecture Notes in Computer Science*, pages 197–208. Springer International Publishing, 2014. DOI: 10.1007/978-3-319-12844-3_17. 7

[136] J. Zhang and J. Huan. Inductive multi-task learning with multiple view data. In *Proc. of the ACM SIGKDD International Conference on Knowledge Discovery and Data Mining*, pages 543–551, 2012. DOI: 10.1145/2339530.2339617. 20, 29, 50, 58, 77

[137] Y. Zhang. Multi-task active learning with output constraints. In *Proc. of the AAAI Conference on Artificial Intelligence*. AAAI Press, 2010. 36

[138] Y. Zhang, J. Tang, Z. Yang, J. Pei, and P. S. Yu. Cosnet: Connecting heterogeneous social networks with local and global consistency. In *Proc. of the ACM SIGKDD International Conference on Knowledge Discovery and Data Mining*, pages 1485–1494, 2015. DOI: 10.1145/2783258.2783268. 7

[139] Y. Zhang and D.-Y. Yeung. A convex formulation for learning task relationships in multi-task learning. In *Proc. of the Conference on Uncertainty in Artificial Intelligence*, pages 733–442. AUAI Press, 2010. 36, 77

[140] Y. Zhang and D.-Y. Yeung. Learning high-order task relationships in multi-task learning. In *Proc. of the International Joint Conference on Artificial Intelligence*, pages 1917–1923. AAAI Press, 2013. 36

[141] Y.-L. Zhao, Q. Chen, S. Yan, T.-S. Chua, and D. Zhang. Detecting profilable and overlapping communities with user-generated multimedia contents in lbsns. *ACM Transactions on Multimedia Computing, Communications, and Applications*, 10:3:1–3:22, 2013. DOI: 10.1145/2502415. 65

[142] Y.-L. Zhao, L. Nie, X. Wang, and T.-S. Chua. Personalized recommendations of locally interesting venues to tourists via cross-region community matching. *ACM Transactions on Intelligent Systems and Technology*, 5(3):50:1–50:26, 2014. DOI: 10.1145/2532439. 10, 75

[143] V. W. Zheng, S. J. Pan, Q. Yang, and J. J. Pan. Transferring multi-device localization models using latent multi-task learning. In *Proc. of the AAAI Conference on Artificial Intelligence*, pages 1427–1432. AAAI Press, 2008. 36

[144] B. Zhou, J. Pei, and W. Luk. A brief survey on anonymization techniques for privacy preserving publishing of social network data. *ACM SIGKDD Explorations Newsletter*, 10, pages 12–22, 2008. DOI: 10.1145/1540276.1540279. 86

[145] J. Zhou, J. Chen, and J. Ye. Clustered multi-task learning via alternating structure optimization. In *Advances in Neural Information Processing Systems*, pages 702–710. MIT Press, 2011. 37, 40, 45

[146] K. Zhou, S.-H. Yang, and H. Zha. Functional matrix factorizations for cold-start recommendation. In *Proc. of the International ACM SIGIR Conference on Research and Development in Information Retrieval*, pages 315–324, 2011. DOI: 10.1145/2009916.2009961. 10

[147] X. Zhu, Z.-Y. Ming, X. Zhu, and T.-S. Chua. Topic hierarchy construction for the organization of multi-source user generated contents. In *Proc. of the International ACM SIGIR Conference on Research and Development in Information Retrieval*, pages 233–242, 2013. DOI: 10.1145/2484028.2484032. 18

Authors' Biographies

LIQIANG NIE

Dr. Liqiang Nie received a B.E. degree from Xi'an Jiaotong University of China, Xi'an, in 2009, and a Ph.D. degree from National University of Singapore, in 2013. Currently, he is a research fellow at the National University of Singapore. His research interests include social network analysis and media search. Various parts of his work have been published in top forums including ACM SIGIR, ACM MM, IJCAI, TOIS, TIST, and TMM. He served as the guest editor and special session chair for several journals and conferences, respectively.

XUEMENG SONG

Xuemeng Song is currently a Ph.D. student at the School of Computing, National University of Singapore. She received her degree from the University of Science and Technology of China in 2012. Her research interests are information retrieval and social network analysis. She has published several papers in top venues, such as SIGIR and TOIS. In addition, she has served as a reviewer for many top conferences and journals.

TAT-SENG CHUA

Dr. Chua is the KITHCT Chair Professor at the School of Computing, National University of Singapore. He was the Acting and Founding Dean of the School during 1998–2000. Dr. Chua's main research interest is in multimedia information retrieval and social media analysis. In particular, his research focuses on the extraction, retrieval and question-answering (QA) of text, video, and live media arising from the Web and social networks. He is the director of a multi-million-dollar joint center (named NExT) between NUS and Tsinghua University in China to develop technologies for live media search. The project will gather, mine, search, and organize user-generated content within the cities of Beijing and Singapore. His group participates regularly in TREC-QA and TRECVID video retrieval evaluations.

Dr. Chua is active in the international research community. He has organized and served as program committee member of numerous international conferences in the areas of computer graphics, multimedia, and text processing. He is the conference co-chair of ACM Multimedia 2005, ACM CIVR 2005, and ACM SIGIR 2008. He serves on the editorial boards of: *ACM Transactions of Information Systems* (ACM), *Foundation and Trends in Information Retrieval* (NOW), *The Visual Computer* (Springer Verlag), and *Multimedia Tools and Applications* (Kluwer). He is a member of the steering committee of ICMR (International Conference on Multimedia Retrieval) and Multimedia Modeling conference series and a member of the international review panel of two large-scale research projects in Europe.

Dr. Chua serves as the Chairman of the Board of Examiners for the Certified IT Project Management ("CITPM") in Singapore. He is the independent Director of two publicly listed companies in Singapore. He holds a Ph.D. from the University of Leeds, UK.